COMPENDIUM OF THE CONFEDERATE ARMIES

ALABAMA

COMPENDIUM OF THE CONFEDERATE ARMIES

ALABAMA

Stewart Sifakis

Facts On File
New York • Oxford

COMPENDIUM OF THE CONFEDERATE ARMIES: ALABAMA

Copyright © 1992 by Stewart Sifakis

Facts On File, Inc.
460 Park Avenue South
New York NY 10016
USA

Facts On File Limited
Collins Street
Oxford OX4 1XJ
United Kingdom

Library of Congress Cataloging-in-Publication Data

Sifakis, Stewart.
  Compendium of the Confederate armies / Stewart Sifakis.
    p. cm.
  Includes bibliographical references and indexes.
  Contents: Virginia—Tennessee—Alabama—Florida and Arkansas—North Carolina
  ISBN 0-8160-2287-9
  1. Confederate States of America. Army—History. 2. United States—History—Civil War, 1861–1865—Regimental histories.
  I. Title.
E546.S58 1991
973.7'42—dc20   90-23631

A British CIP catalogue record for this book is available from the British Library.

Facts On File books are available at special discounts when purchased in bulk quantities for businesses, associations, institutions or sales promotions. Please call our Special Sales Department in New York at 212/683-2244 (dial 800/322-8755 except in NY, AK, or HI) or in Oxford at 865/728399.

Text design by Ron Monteleone
Composition by the Maple-Vail Book Manufacturing Group
Manufactured by the Maple-Vail Book Manufacturing Group
Printed in the United States of America

10 9 8 7 6 5 4 3 2 1

This book is printed on acid-free paper.

To
the Memory of James Sifakis
1893–1961

CONTENTS

ACKNOWLEDGMENTS

I am deeply indebted for this work to the personnel, past and present, of Facts On File, especially to Edward Knappman, Gerry Helferich, and my editors: Kate Kelly, Helen Flynn, Eleanora vonDehsen, Traci Cothran and Nicholas Bakalar. Also I would like to thank the staffs of the National Archives, Library of Congress, the various state archives and the New York Public Library for their patience and assistance. Over the past decades the staff of the National Park Service, Edwin C. Bearss, chief historian, have proven very informative on my frequent visits to the various battlefields. To Shaun Potter, Christina Villano and Sally Gadsby I am indebted for keeping me at my work. For the logistical support of the management of the Hotel Post, Zermatt (Karl Ivarsson, Ursula Waeny and Leslie Dawkins), I am very grateful. And last, but certainly not least, I owe thanks to John Warren for his knowledge of computers, without which this project would have ground to a halt, and to his computer widow, Evelyne.

INTRODUCTION

This work is intended to be the companion set to Frederick H. Dyer's *Compendium of the War of the Rebellion* for the Confederacy. The Compendium was first published as a three-volume work in 1909. A study of all the Union regiments, battalions, batteries and independent companies, it has since been reprinted in two- and one-volume editions.

It has been estimated that for every day since the end of the American Civil War, one book, magazine or newspaper article has appeared dealing with some aspect of that fratricidal struggle. Many ask: If so much has been written on the Civil War, is there really a need for more? The answer is an emphatic yes. Many aspects of the conflict have been covered only superficially and require much more in-depth research. But for such research a bedrock of reference works is essential.

There are many such works available, including the U.S. War Department's 128-volume *The War of the Rebellion: A Compilation of the Official Records of the Union and Confederate Armies* and the U.S. Navy Department's 31-volume *Official Records of the Union and Confederate Navies in the War of the Rebellion.* Registers of military personnel include: George W. Cullum's two-volume *Biographical Register of the Officers and Graduates of the United States Military Academy*, Francis B. Heitman's two-volume *Historical Register and Dictionary of the United States Army From Its Organization, September 29, 1789, to March 2, 1903*, Guy V. Henry's two-volume *Military Record of Civilian Appointments in the United States Army*, Robert K. Krick's *Lee's Colonels: A Biographical Register of the Field Officers of the Army of Northern Virginia* and Ezra J. Warner's *Generals in Gray: Lives of the Confederate Commanders* and *Generals in Blue: Lives of the Union Commanders*. Politics are covered in Jon L. Wakelyn's *Biographical Dictionary of the Confederacy* and Ezra J. Warner's and W. Buck Yearns' *Biographical Register of the Confederate Congress*. E. B. Long's *The Civil War Day by Day: An Almanac 1861-1865* provides an excellent chronology. Collective biographies include Mark M. Boatner's *The Civil War Dictionary*, Patricia L. Faust's *Historical Times Illustrated Encyclopedia of the Civil War* and Stewart

Sifakis' *Who Was Who in the Civil War*. Then, of course there is Dyer's Compendium.

To date there has not been a comprehensive equivalent to Dyer's work for the South as a whole. Basically work has been done by individual states. North Carolina has an excellent work currently nearing completion. Other commendable works have been done for Tennessee, Virginia and Texas. Works were begun for Georgia and South Carolina but did not proceed far. State government agencies in Florida and Kentucky made some efforts in the early years after the war. However, none of these draws a consolidated picture of the Confederate States Army. That is where the *Compendium of the Confederate Armies* comes in.

This work is organized into volumes by state. One volume includes the border state units—Kentucky, Maryland and Missouri; units organized directly by the Confederate authorities from various state companies; and those units from the Indian nations allied with the Confederacy. The final volume consists of the tables of organization of the various armies and departments throughout the war.

There are chapters in each volume on the artillery, cavalry and infantry. Those units having a numerical designation are listed first, followed by those units using the name of their commander, home region or some other name. Units are then broken down alphabetically by size—for example, battalions, batteries, companies and regiments. If two or more units still have the same sorting features, they are then further broken down alphabetically by any special designation—1st or 2nd Organization, Local Defense Troops, Militia, Provisional Army, Regulars, Reserves, Sharpshooters, State Guard, State Line, State Troops or Volunteers and so on. The company designation for artillery batteries that served within an artillery battalion or regiment is listed at the end of the battalion or regiment designation. If heavy artillery battalions or regiments served together as a unit through most of the war, they are treated as a whole with no breakdown of the companies.

Each entry starts with the unit's name. Any nicknames or other mistaken designations follow. Then comes a summary of its organizational details: its date and location of organization, mustering into service, the number of companies for battalion organizations, armament for artillery batteries, surrenders, paroles, exchanges and disbandment or mustering out. The next paragraph starts with the first commanding officer and continues with an alphabetical listing of the other field-grade officers. (Captains are listed chronologically for artillery batteries.) The next paragraph is the brigade and higher-level command assignments of the unit. This is followed by a listing of the battles and campaigns the unit was engaged in. Note that the unit was not necessarily present on each date that is indicated for multiday actions. The final paragraph is the suggested further reading, if any.

Because records are incomplete, I have dropped the list of casualties of each unit that Dyer includes for the Northern units. But I have added to Dyer's format by including the first commanding officer and the field-grade officers of each unit. Selected bibliographies are included for each volume. Also, as available, unit histories and personal memoirs are listed with some units as suggested further reading.

ALABAMA UNITS

Alabama seceded from the Union on January 11, 1861. Upon the creation of the Confederate Army, Alabama's troops were incorporated into it.

Several specialized types of units were organized for the army. The Confederate Congress passed an act authorizing the creation of Local Defense Troops units on August 21, 1861. However, the Confederate Adjutant and Inspector General's Office did not issue its General Orders #86 outlining the regulations for their organization until June 23, 1863. These units were usually organized on the company and battalion level for defense of the areas in which they were raised. Often they were composed of employees of government arsenals, armories, bureaus and so on or from men detailed from regular line units for detached service. Toward the end of the war, some of these units were organized into regiments that were to be called into active service only when the situation in their vicinity required it.

The Confederate Congress created the Reserves on February 17, 1864, when it expanded conscription to include all white males between 17 and 50 years of age. Those under 18 and those over 45 were to be organized in the Reserves, troops that did not have to serve beyond the boundaries of the state.

ARTILLERY

1. ALABAMA 1ST ARTILLERY BATTALION

Organization: Organized in March 1861. Mustered into Confederate service for three years on May 24, 1861.
First Commander: James T. Gee (Major, Lieutenant Colonel)
Field Officer: Robert C. Forsyth (Major)

2. ALABAMA 1ST ARTILLERY BATTALION, COMPANY A

Organization: Organized on January 19, 1861. Mustered into Confederate service for three years on May 24, 1861. Armed with two 6-lb. Smoothbores on October 31, 1861. Surrendered at Fort Morgan, Alabama, on August 22, 1864.
First Commander: William Walker (Captain)
Captain: William B. Hughes
Assignments: Mobile (May-October 1861)
District of Alabama, Department of Alabama and West Florida (October 1861-January 1862)
Army of Mobile, Department of Alabama and West Florida (January-June 1862)
Powell's Brigade, District of the Gulf, Department #2 (July 1862-April 1863)
Powell's-Shoup's-Higgins' Brigade, Department of the Gulf (April 1863-April 1864)
Page's Brigade, District of the Gulf, Department of Alabama, Mississippi and East Louisiana (April-August 1864)
Battle: Mobile Bay (August 1864)

3. ALABAMA 1ST ARTILLERY BATTALION, COMPANY B

Organization: Organized on January 29, 1861. Mustered into Confederate service for three years on May 24, 1861. Surrendered at Fort Gaines, Alabama, on August 7, 1861.
First Commander: Stephen P. Winston (Captain)

Captain: William Wellborn
Assignments: Mobile (May-October 1861)
District of Alabama, Department of Alabama and West Florida (October 1861-January 1862)
Army of Mobile, Department of Alabama and West Florida (January-June 1862)
Powell's Brigade, District of the Gulf, Department #2 (July 1862-April 1863)
Powell's-Shoup's-Higgins' Brigade, Department of the Gulf (April 1863-April 1864)
Page's Brigade, District of the Gulf, Department of Alabama, Mississippi and East Louisiana (April-August 1864)
Battle: Mobile Bay (August 1864)

4. ALABAMA 1ST ARTILLERY BATTALION, COMPANY C

Organization: Organized on January 29, 1861. Mustered into Confederate service for three years on May 24, 1861. Surrendered at Fort Morgan, Alabama, on August 22, 1864.
First Commander: Joseph M. Cary (Captain)
Assignments: Mobile (May-October 1861)
District of Alabama, Department of Alabama and West Florida (October 1861-January 1862)
Army of Mobile, Department of Alabama and West Florida (January-June 1862)
Powell's Brigade, District of the Gulf, Department #2 (July 1862-April 1863)
Powell's-Shoup's-Higgins' Brigade, Department of the Gulf (April 1863-April 1864)
Page's Brigade, District of the Gulf, Department of Alabama, Mississippi and East Louisiana (April-August 1864)
Battle: Mobile Bay (August 1864)

5. ALABAMA 1ST ARTILLERY BATTALION, COMPANY D

Organization: Organized on January 29, 1861. Mustered into Confederate service for three years on May 24, 1861. Surrendered at Fort Gaines, Alabama, on August 7, 1864.
First Commander: Junius A. Law (Captain)
Assignments: Mobile (May-October 1861)
District of Alabama, Department of Alabama and West Florida (October 1861-January 1862)
Army of Mobile, Department of Alabama and West Florida (January-June 1862)
Powell's Brigade, District of the Gulf, Department #2 (July 1862-April 1863)

Powell's-Shoup's-Higgins' Brigade, Department of the Gulf (April 1863-April 1864)

Page's Brigade, District of the Gulf, Department of Alabama, Mississippi and East Louisiana (April-August 1864)

Battle: Mobile Bay (August 1864)

6. ALABAMA 1ST ARTILLERY BATTALION, COMPANY E

Organization: Organized on February 23, 1861. Mustered into Confederate service for three years on May 24, 1861. Surrendered at Fort Morgan, Alabama, on August 22, 1864.

First Commander: John Q. Loomis (Captain)

Captains: William R. Julian

Robert M. Campbell

Assignments: Mobile (May-October 1861)

District of Alabama, Department of Alabama and West Florida (October 1861-January 1862)

Army of Mobile, Department of Alabama and West Florida (January-June 1862)

Powell's Brigade, District of the Gulf, Department #2 (July 1862-April 1863)

Powell's-Shoup's-Higgins' Brigade, Department of the Gulf (April 1863-April 1864)

Page's Brigade, District of the Gulf, Department of Alabama, Mississippi and East Louisiana (April-August 1864)

Battle: Mobile Bay (August 1864)

7. ALABAMA 1ST ARTILLERY BATTALION, COMPANY F

Organization: Organized on January 23, 1861. Mustered into Confederate service for three years on May 24, 1861. Surrendered at Fort Morgan, Alabama, on August 22, 1864.

First Commander: Edward Wallace (Captain)

Captain: J. W. Whiting

Assignments: Mobile (May-October 1861)

District of Alabama, Department of Alabama and West Florida (October 1861-January 1862)

Army of Mobile, Department of Alabama and West Florida (January-June 1862)

Powell's Brigade, District of the Gulf, Department #2 (July 1862-April 1863)

Powell's-Shoup's-Higgins' Brigade, Department of the Gulf (April 1863-April 1864)

Page's Brigade, District of the Gulf, Department of Alabama, Mississippi and East Louisiana (April-August 1864)

Battle: Mobile Bay (August 1864)

8. ALABAMA 2ND LIGHT ARTILLERY BATTALION

Organization: Organized on December 12, 1861. Surrendered at various locations between April 26, 1865, and May 4, 1865.
First Commander: James H. Hollinquist (Major, Lieutenant Colonel)

9. ALABAMA 2ND LIGHT ARTILLERY BATTALION, COMPANY A

Nickname: McRae Light Artillery
Organization: Organized on October 17, 1861. Mustered in on October 17, 1861. Armed with four 6-lb. Smoothbores between November 28, 1863, and January 5, 1864. Armed with four 12-lb. Napoleons between May 1, 1864 and February 21, 1865. Surrendered by Lieutenant Richard Taylor, commanding the Department of Alabama, Mississippi and East Louisiana, at Citronelle, Alabama, on May 4, 1865.
First Commander: Stephen Charpentier (Captain)
Captain: John M. Jenks
Assignments: District of Alabama, Department of Alabama and West Florida (November 1861-January 1862)
Army of Mobile, Department of Alabama and West Florida (January-June 1862)
Army of Mobile, District of the Gulf, Department #2 (July-November 1862)
Slaughter's Brigade, Western Division, Department of the Gulf (April-May 1863)
Featherston's Brigade, Loring's Division, Department of the West (May-July 1863)
Featherston's Brigade, Loring's Division, Department of Mississippi and East Louisiana (July 1863-January 1864)
Featherston's Brigade, Loring's Division, Department of Alabama, Mississippi and East Louisiana (January-February 1864)
Artillery Battalion, Loring's Division, Department of Alabama, Mississippi and East Louisiana (March-May 1864)
Artillery Battalion, Loring's Division, Army of Mississippi (May 1864)
Armistead's Cavalry Brigade, District of Central and North Alabama, Department of Alabama, Mississippi and East Louisiana (August 1864)
Artillery, District of Central and North Alabama, Department of Alabama, Mississippi and East Louisiana (August-October 1864)
Semple's Artillery Battalion, District of the Gulf, Department of Alabama, Mississippi and East Louisiana (October 1864-February 1865)
Artillery, District of Central Alabama, Department of Alabama, Mississippi and East Louisiana (February-May 1865)

Battles: Jackson Siege (July 1863)
Meridian Campaign (February-March 1864)
Atlanta Campaign (May-September 1864)
New Hope Church (May 25-June 4, 1864)

10. ALABAMA 2ND LIGHT ARTILLERY BATTALION, COMPANY B

Organization: Organized at Mobile on October 16, 1861. Mustered in on October 31, 1861. Broken up with some of the enlisted men transferred to Cobb's Kentucky Artillery Battery in January 1864.
First Commander: David D. Waters (Captain)
Assignments: District of Alabama, Department of Alabama and West Florida (December 1861-January 1862)
Army of Mobile, Department of Alabama and West Florida (January-April 1862)
Trapier's-Manigault's Brigade, Withers' Division, 2nd Corps, Army of the Mississippi, Department #2 (April-June 1862)
Manigault's Brigade, Reserve Corps, Army of the Mississippi, Department #2 (June-July 1862)
Manigault's Brigade, Reserve Division, Army of the Mississippi, Department #2 (July-August 1862)
Manigault's Brigade, Withers' Division, Right Wing, Army of the Mississippi, Department #2 (August-November 1862)
Manigault's Brigade, Withers'-Hindman's Division, 1st Corps, Army of Tennessee (November 1862-September 1863)
Artillery Battalion, Hindman's Division, 1st Corps, Army of Tennessee (November-December 1863)
Atlanta, Georgia, Department of Tennessee (December 1863-January 1864)
Battles: Munfordville (September 17, 1862)
Murfreesboro (December 31, 1862-January 3, 1863)
Tullahoma Campaign (June 1863)
Chickamauga (September 19-20, 1863)
Chattanooga Siege (September-November 1863)
Chattanooga (November 23-25, 1863)

11. ALABAMA 2ND LIGHT ARTILLERY BATTALION, COMPANY C

Organization: Organized and mustered in on November 1, 1861. Regiment surrendered at Vicksburg, Mississippi on July 4, 1863. Paroled there later in month. Surrendered by Lieutenant Richard Taylor, commanding the Department of Alabama, Mississippi and East Louisiana, at Citronelle, Alabama, on May 4, 1865.
First Commander: John D. Haynie (Captain)

Captains: Thomas K. Emanuel
John R. Sclator
Assignments: District of Alabama, Department of Alabama and West Florida (December 1861-January 1862)
Army of Mobile, Department of Alabama and West Florida (January-June 1862)
Army of Mobile, District of the Gulf, Department #2 (July 1862)
Hébert's Brigade, Maury's-Forney's Division, Department of Mississippi and East Louisiana (April-July 1863)
Forney's Command, Department of Mississippi and East Louisiana (November 1863-May 1864)
Burnet's Command, Artillery Reserves, etc., District of the Gulf, Department of Alabama, Mississippi and East Louisiana (March-April 1865)
Burnet's Command, Department of Alabama, Mississippi and East Louisiana (April-May 1865)
Battles: Vicksburg Campaign (May-July 1863)
Vicksburg Siege (May-July 1863)
Mobile (March 17-April 12, 1865)

12.   ALABAMA 2ND LIGHT ARTILLERY BATTALION, COMPANY D

Organization: Organized at Mobile on November 8, 1861. Regiment surrendered at Vicksburg, Mississippi on July 4, 1863. Paroled there later in month. Declared exchanged in November 1863. Broken up and enlisted men assigned to Barret's Missouri Artillery Battery on November 19, 1863.
First Commander: Henry H. Sengstak (Captain)
Assignments: District of Alabama, Department of Alabama and West Florida (December 1861-January 1862)
Army of Mobile, Department of Alabama and West Florida (January-June 1862)
Army of Mobile, District of the Gulf, Department #2 (July 1862)
Reserve Artillery, Price's Corps, Army of West Tennessee, Department of Mississippi and East Louisiana (October 1862)
Reserve Artillery, 2nd Corps, Army of North Mississippi, Department of Mississippi and East Louisiana (December 1862-January 1863)
Artillery, Maury's Division, 2nd Military District, Department of Mississippi and East Louisiana (January-April 1863)
Moore's Brigade, Maury's-Forney's Division, Department of Mississippi and East Louisiana (April-July 1863)
Robertson's Battalion, Reserve Artillery, Army of Tennessee (November 1863)
Battles: Corinth (October 3-4, 1862)
vs. Steele's Bayou Expedition (March 14-27, 1863)

vs. Steele's Greenville Expedition (April 2-25, 1863)
Thomas' Plantation, Mississippi (section) (April 7, 1863)
Vicksburg Campaign (May-July 1863)
Champion Hill (detachment) (May 16, 1863)
Vicksburg Siege (May-July 1863)

13. ALABAMA 2ND LIGHT ARTILLERY BATTALION, COMPANY E

Organization: Organized at Mobile on October 10, 1861. Reorganized on April 28, 1862. Armed with two 3-inch Rifles and two 12-lb. Howitzers on April 6-7, 1862. Surrendered by Lieutenant Richard Taylor, commanding the Department of Alabama, Mississippi and East Louisiana, at Meridian, Mississippi, on May 4, 1865.
First Commander: Charles P. Gage (Captain)
Captains: James H. Hill
James H. Hutchinsson
Assignments: District of Alabama, Department of Alabama and West Florida (October 1861-January 1862)
Army of Mobile, Department of Alabama and West Florida (January-March 1862)
Mouton's Brigade, 1st Corps, 2nd Grand Division, Army of the Mississippi, Department #2 (March 1862)
Chalmers' Brigade, Withers' Division, 2nd Corps, Army of the Mississippi, Department #2 (March-April 1862)
Army of Mobile, Department of Alabama and West Florida (June 1862)
Army of Mobile, District of the Gulf, Department #2 (July 1862-June 1863)
Slaughter's Brigade, Department of the Gulf (June 1863)
Cantey's Brigade, Western Division, Department of the Gulf (July-August 1863)
Cantey's Brigade, Department of the Gulf (August 1863)
Bay Batteries, Department of the Gulf (September 1863-April 1864)
Bay Batteries, Higgins' Brigade, District of the Gulf, Department of Alabama, Mississippi and East Louisiana (April-October 1864)
Bay Batteries, District of the Gulf, Department of Alabama, Mississippi and East Louisiana (October 1864-April 1865)
Maury's Command, Department of Alabama, Mississippi and East Louisiana (April-May 1865)
Battles: Shiloh (April 6-7, 1862)
Mobile (March 17-April 12, 1865)

14. ALABAMA 2ND LIGHT ARTILLERY BATTALION, COMPANY F

Organization: Organized at Tuscaloosa on November 29, 1861. Armed with four 12-lb. Napoleons between March 29, 1864, and December 16, 1864. Surrendered by Lieutenant Richard Taylor, commanding the Department of

Alabama, Mississippi and East Louisiana, at Citronelle, Alabama, on May 4, 1865.

First Commander: Charles L. Lumsden (Captain)

Assignments: District of Alabama, Department of Alabama and West Florida (November 1861-January 1862)

Army of Mobile, Department of Alabama and West Florida (January-April 1862)

Chalmers' Brigade, Withers' Division, 2nd Corps, Army of the Mississippi, Department #2 (April-June 1862)

L. M. Walker's Brigade, 2nd Corps, Army of the Mississippi, Department #2 (June-July 1862)

Jones'-Anderson's Division, Army of the Mississippi, Department #2 (July-August 1862)

T. M. Jones' Brigade, Anderson's Division, Left Wing, Army of the Mississippi, Department #2 (August-November 1862)

T. M. Jones' Brigade, Anderson's Division, 2nd Corps, Army of Tennessee (November-December 1862)

Reserve Artillery, Army of Tennessee (December 1862-November 1863)

Robertson's Battalion, Reserve Artillery, Army of Tennessee (November 1863-April 1864)

Palmer's Battalion, Reserve Artillery, Army of Tennessee (April-July 1864)

Palmer's Battalion, Artillery, 1st Corps, Army of Tennessee (July-September 1864)

Palmer's Artillery Battalion, Macon, Georgia, Army of Tennessee (September 1864)

Truehart's Battalion, Artillery, 3rd Corps, Army of Tennessee (December 1864-January 1865)

Truehart's Artillery Battalion, Right Wing, Defenses of Mobile, Artillery Reserves, etc., Department of Alabama, Mississippi and East Louisiana (March-April 1865)

Truehart's Artillery Battalion, Smith's Regiment, Department of Alabama, Mississippi and East Louisiana (April-May 1865)

Battles: Corinth Campaign (April-June 1862)

Farmington (May 1862)

Perryville (October 8, 1862)

Murfreesboro (December 31, 1862-January 3, 1863)

Tullahoma Campaign (June 1863)

Chickamauga (September 19-20, 1863)

Chattanooga Siege (September-November 1863)

Chattanooga (November 23-25, 1863)

Atlanta Campaign (May-September 1864)

Kennesaw Mountain (June 27, 1864)

Atlanta Siege (July-September 1864)
Nashville (December 15-16, 1864)
Mobile (March 17-April 12, 1865)
Further Reading: Little, Dr. George, and Maxwell, James R. A *History of Lumsden's Battery*, C.S.A.

15. ALABAMA 20TH LIGHT ARTILLERY BATTALION

Organization: Organized by the division of Waddell's Artillery Battery in October 1863.
First Commander: James F. Waddell (Major)

16. ALABAMA 20TH LIGHT ARTILLERY BATTALION, COMPANY A

Organization: Organized from part of Waddell's Artillery Battery in October 1863. Armed with four 10-lb. Parrotts on March 29, 1864. Final disposition uncertain.
First Commander: Winslow D. Emery (Captain)
Assignments: Waddell's Battalion, Reserve Artillery, Army of Tennessee (February-July 1864)
Waddell's Battalion, Artillery, 3rd Corps, Army of Tennessee (July-September 1864)
Waddell's Artillery Battalion, Macon, Georgia, Army of Tennessee (September 1864)
Battles: Atlanta Campaign (May-September 1864)
Atlanta Siege (July-September 1864)

17. ALABAMA 20TH LIGHT ARTILLERY BATTALION, COMPANY B

Organization: Organized from part of Waddell's Artillery Battery in October 1863. Armed with two 6-lb. Blakeleys and two 12-lb. Blakeleys on March 29, 1864. Final disposition uncertain.
First Commander: Richard H. Bellamy (Captain)
Assignments: Waddell's Battalion, Reserve Artillery, Army of Tennessee (February-July 1864)
Waddell's Battalion, Artillery, 3rd Corps, Army of Tennessee (July-September 1864)
Waddell's Artillery Battalion, Macon, Georgia, Army of Tennessee (September 1864)
Battles: Atlanta Campaign (May-September 1864)
Atlanta Siege (July-September 1864)

18. ALABAMA 20TH LIGHT ARTILLERY BATTALION, COMPANY C

See: ARKANSAS HELENA ARTILLERY

19. ALABAMA BARBOUR ARTILLERY BATTERY

Organization: Organized as Company C, 4th Artillery Battalion, Hilliard's Legion, in April 1862. Mustered into Confederate service at Eufaula on April 30, 1862. Armed with two 6-lb. Smoothbores and two 12-lb. Howitzers on March 29, 1864. Surrendered at Augusta, Georgia, in April 1865.

First Commander: William N. Reeves (Captain)

Captain: R. F. Kolb

Assignments: Hilliard's Legion, McCown's Division, Department of East Tennessee (October-November 1862)

Hilliard's Legion, Heth's Division, Department of East Tennessee (November-December 1862)

Palmer's-Frazer's Brigade, Department of East Tennessee (December 1862-July 1863)

Frazer's Brigade, Army of East Tennessee, Department of Tennessee (July-August 1863)

Reserve Artillery, Buckner's Corps, Army of Tennessee (August-September 1863)

Artillery Battalion, Buckner's Division, Longstreet's Corps, Army of Tennessee (September-October 1863)

Artillery Battalion, Buckner's Division, 1st Corps, Army of Tennessee (October-November 1863)

Williams' Battalion, Reserve Artillery, Army of Tennessee (November 1863-July 1864)

Williams' Battalion, Artillery, 2nd Corps, Army of Tennessee (July-September 1864)

Williams' Artillery Battalion, Macon, Georgia, Army of Tennessee (September 1864)

District of Georgia, Department of Tennessee and Georgia (presumably) (April 1865)

Battles: Chickamauga (September 19-20, 1863)

Chattanooga Siege (September-November 1863)

Chattanooga (November 23-25, 1863)

Atlanta Campaign (May-September 1864)

New Hope Church (May 25-June 4, 1864)

Atlanta Siege (July-September 1864)

Nashville (December 15-16, 1864)

20. ALABAMA EUFAULA ARTILLERY BATTERY

Organization: Organized and mustered into Confederate service at Eufaula on February 26, 1862. Battery still unarmed on April 10, 1862. Armed with four 3-inch Rifles on March 29, 1864. Surrendered by Lieutenant Richard Taylor, commanding the Department of Alabama, Mississippi and East Louisiana, at Citronelle, Alabama, on May 4, 1865.

First Commander: John W. Clark (Captain)

Captains: William A. McTyer
McDonald Oliver
William J. McKenzie

Assignments: Department of East Tennessee (April 1862)
Stevenson' Brigade, Department of East Tennessee (April-July 1862)
Rains' Brigade, Stevenson's Division, Department of East Tennessee (October-December 1862)
Rains'-Vance's Brigade, McCown's Division, Department of East Tennessee (December 1862-March 1863)
Vance's-Bate's Brigade, McCown's-Stewart's Division, 1st Corps, Army of Tennessee (March-June 1863)
Bate's Brigade, Stewart's Division, 2nd Corps, Army of Tennessee (June-August 1863)
Artillery Battalion, Stewart's Division, 2nd Corps, Army of Tennessee (August-September 1863)
Artillery Battalion, Stewart's Division, Buckner's Corps, Army of Tennessee (September 1863)
Artillery Battalion, Stewart's Division, 2nd Corps, Army of Tennessee (September 1863-February 1864)
Eldridge's Battalion, 2nd Corps, Army of Tennessee (February 1864-January 1865)
Hoxton's Artillery Battalion, Left Wing, Defenses of Mobile, Artillery Reserves, etc., Department of Alabama, Mississippi and East Louisiana (March-April 1865)
Hoxton's Artillery Battalion, Fuller's Regiment, Department of Alabama, Mississippi and East Louisiana (April-May 1865)

Battles: Murfreesboro (December 31, 1862-January 3, 1863)
Tullahoma Campaign (June 1863)
Hoover's Gap (June 24, 1863)
Chickamauga (September 19-20, 1863)
Chattanooga Siege (September-November 1863)
Chattanooga (November 23-25, 1863)
Atlanta Campaign (May-September 1864)
New Hope Church (May 25-June 4, 1864)
Atlanta Siege (July-September 1864)
Nashville (December 15-16, 1864)
Mobile (March 17-April 12, 1865)

21. ALABAMA FOWLER'S-PHELAN'S ARTILLERY BATTERY

Organization: Organized by the conversion of Company H, 5th Infantry Regiment, to artillery service at Davis Ford, Virginia, on December 28, 1861.

Mustered in on April 14, 1862 to date from December 28, 1861. Armed with four 12-lb. Napoleons from December 14, 1863 to March 29, 1864. Surrendered by Lieutenant Richard Taylor, commanding the Department of Alabama, Mississippi and East Louisiana, at Citronelle, Alabama, on May 4, 1865.

First Commander: William H. Fowler (Captain)

Captain: John Phelan

Assignments: On furlough (January-March 1862)

Army of Mobile, Department of Alabama and West Florida (March-June 1862)

Department #2 (June-July 1862)

District of the Gulf, Department #2 (July 1862)

Detachment of Observation, District of the Gulf, Department #2 (October-November 1862)

Cumming's Brigade, Western Division (Mackall), Department of the Gulf (April-May 1863)

Walthall's Brigade, Withers' Division, 1st Corps, Army of Tennessee (July-August 1863)

Artillery Battalion, Liddell's Division, Reserve Corps, Army of Tennessee (September 1863)

Fowler's Battalion, Artillery, 1st Corps, Army of Tennessee (October-November 1863)

Artillery Battalion, Cheatham's Division, 1st Corps, Army of Tennessee (November 1863-February 1864)

Hoxton's Battalion, Artillery, 1st Corps, Army of Tennessee (February 1864-February 1865)

Gee's Artillery Battalion, Right Wing, Defenses of Mobile, Artillery Reserves, etc., Department of Alabama, Mississippi and East Louisiana (March-April 1865)

3rd Battalion, Smith's Brigade, Department of Alabama, Mississippi and East Louisiana (April-May 1865)

Battles: Tullahoma Campaign (June 1863)

Chickamauga (September 19-20, 1863)

Chattanooga Siege (September-November 1863)

Chattanooga (November 23-25, 1863)

Atlanta Campaign (May-September 1864)

Resaca (May 14-15, 1864)

Atlanta Siege (July-September 1864)

Franklin (November 30, 1864)

Nashville (December 15-16, 1864)

Mobile (March 17-April 12, 1865)

22. ALABAMA GARRITY'S ARTILLERY BATTERY

See: ALABAMA STATE ARTILLERY BATTERY

23. ALABAMA GID. NELSON ARTILLERY BATTERY

Organization: Organized at Uniontown on May 2, 1862. Armed with four 20-lb. Parrotts and four 12-lb. Howitzers on January 11, 1864. Surrendered by Lieutenant Richard Taylor, commanding the Department of Alabama, Mississippi and East Louisiana, at Citronelle, Alabama, on May 4, 1865.

First Commander: Joseph J. Selden (Captain)

Captain: Charles W. Lovelace

Assignments: Army of Mobile, District of the Gulf, Department #2 (October 1862-April 1863)

Slaughter's-Cantey's Brigade, Western Division, Department of the Gulf (April-August 1863)

Eastern Division, Department of the Gulf (one section) (June-August 1863)

Amerine's Brigade, Department of the Gulf (one section) (August-September 1863)

Truehart's Artillery Battalion, Cantey's Brigade, Department of the Gulf (August 1863-January 1864)

Truehart's Artillery Battalion, Shoup's-Fuller's Artillery Brigade, Department of the Gulf (February-April 1864)

Truehart's Artillery Battalion, Fuller's Artillery Brigade, District of the Gulf, Department of Alabama, Mississippi and East Louisiana (April-May 1864)

Artillery Battalion, Cantey's-Walthall's Division, Army of Mississippi (May-July 1864)

Preston's-Truehart's Battalion, Artillery, Army of Mississippi (July 1864)

Truehart's Battalion, 3rd Corps, Army of Tennessee (July 1864-January 1865)

Truehart's Artillery Battalion, Right Wing, Defenses of Mobile, Artillery Reserves, etc., Department of Alabama, Mississippi and East Louisiana (March-April 1865)

Truehart's Artillery Battalion, Smith's Regiment, Department of Alabama, Mississippi and East Louisiana (April-May 1865)

Battles: Atlanta Campaign (May-September 1864)

Kennesaw Mountain (June 27, 1864)

Peach Tree Creek (July 20, 1864)

Atlanta Siege (July-September 1864)

Tilton (October 13, 1864)

Nashville (December 15-16, 1864)

Mobile (March 17-April 12, 1865)

24. ALABAMA HARDAWAY'S-HURT'S ARTILLERY BATTERY

Organization: Organized on June 1, 1861. Mustered into Confederate service for the war at Lynchburg, Virginia, on June 21, 1861. Armed with two 3-inch Rifles and one 2.75-inch Whitworth on September 17, 1862. Armed with one

8-inch Howitzer, two 3-inch Rifles, and one 12-lb. Whitworth on December 28-30, 1864. Surrendered at Appomattox Court House, Virginia, on April 9, 1865.

First Commander: Robert A. Hardaway (Captain)

Captain: William B. Hurt

Assignments: Anderson's Brigade, D. H. Hill's Division, Army of Northern Virginia (May-July 1862)

Artillery Battalion, D. H. Hill's Division, Army of Northern Virginia (July-September 1862)

Artillery Battalion, D. H. Hill's Division, 2nd Corps, Army of Northern Virginia (September 1862-February 1863)

Hardaway's-McIntosh's Battalion, Artillery Reserve, 2nd Corps, Army of Northern Virginia (February-May 1863)

McIntosh's Battalion, Artillery Reserve, 3rd Corps, Army of Northern Virginia (May-July 1863)

McIntosh's Battalion, Artillery, 3rd Corps, Army of Northern Virginia (July 1863-April 1865)

Battles: Seven Pines (May 31-June 1, 1862)

Seven Days Battles (June 25-July 1, 1862)

Antietam (September 17, 1862)

Port Royal (December 4, 1862)

Fredericksburg (December 13, 1862)

Chancellorsville (May 1-4, 1863)

Gettysburg (July 1-3, 1863)

Bristoe Station (October 14, 1863)

Mine Run Campaign (November-December 1863)

The Wilderness (May 5-6, 1864)

Spotsylvania Court House (May 8-21, 1864)

North Anna (May 23-26, 1864)

Cold Harbor (June 1-3, 1864)

Petersburg Siege (June 1864-April 1865)

Appomattox Court House (April 9, 1865)

25. ALABAMA JEFF. DAVIS ARTILLERY BATTERY

Organization: Organized as a cavalry company at Selma in May 1861. Mustered into Confederate service for the war on July 27, 1861. Armed with two 3-inch Rifles and two 12-lb. Howitzers between August 20, 1862 and September 24, 1862. Armed with four 3-inch Rifles on July 1-3, 1863. Surrendered at Appomattox Court House, Virginia, on April 9, 1865.

First Commander: Joseph T. Montgomery (Captain)

Captains: Robert F. Beckham (declined)

James W. Bondurant

William J. Reese

Assignments: Early's Brigade, Van Dorn's-D. H. Hill's Division, Potomac District, Department of Northern Virginia (January-March 1862)

Early's-Garland's Brigade, D. H. Hill's Division, Army of Northern Virginia (March-July 1862)

Artillery Battalion, D. H. Hill's Division, Army of Northern Virginia (July-September 1862)

Artillery Battalion, D. H. Hill's-Rodes' Division, 2nd Corps, Army of Northern Virginia (September 1862-July 1863)

Carter's-Page's Battalion, Artillery, 2nd Corps, Army of Northern Virginia (July 1863-June 1864)

Page's Battalion, Artillery, Valley District, Department of Northern Virginia (June 1864-February 1865)

Cutshaw's Battalion, Artillery, 2nd Corps, Army of Northern Virginia (February-April 1865)

Battles: Yorktown Siege (April-May 1862)

Seven Pines (May 31-June 1, 1862)

Seven Days Battles (June 25-July 1, 1862)

Mechanicsville (June 26, 1862)

Gaines' Mill (June 27, 1862)

Malvern Hill (July 1, 1862)

South Mountain (September 14, 1862)

Antietam (September 17, 1862)

Fredericksburg (December 13, 1862)

Chancellorsville (May 1-4, 1863)

Gettysburg (July 1-3, 1863)

Orange Court House (September 22, 1863)

Bristoe Campaign (October 1863)

Mine Run Campaign (November-December 1863)

The Wilderness (May 5-6, 1864)

Spotsylvania Court House (May 8-21, 1864)

North Anna (May 23-26, 1864)

Cold Harbor (June 1-3, 1864)

Petersburg Siege (June 1864-April 1865)

Fort Clifton (May 9, 1864)

Appomattox Court House (April 9, 1865)

26. ALABAMA KETCHUM'S ARTILLERY BATTERY

See: ALABAMA STATE ARTILLERY BATTERY

27. ALABAMA MCRAE LIGHT ARTILLERY BATTERY

See: ALABAMA 2ND LIGHT ARTILLERY BATTALION, COMPANY A

28. ALABAMA MCWHORTER'S-CLANTON'S ARTILLERY BATTERY

Organization: Organized in Montgomery County in March 1863. Mustered in on March 12, 1863. Armed with one 12-lb. Howitzer and three 6-lb. Smoothbores on January 11, 1864. One section armed with one 10-lb. Parrott and one 12-lb. Howitzer on February 21, 1865. Captured near Columbus, Georgia, on April 16, 1865.

First Commander: Eliphat McWhorter (Captain)

Captain: N. H. Clanton

Assignments: Clanton's Brigade, Western Division, Department of the Gulf (July-August 1863)

Clanton's Brigade, Department of the Gulf (September 1863)

Eastern Division (Clanton), Department of the Gulf (September 1863)

Clanton's Brigade, Department of the Gulf (February-September 1864)

Clanton's Cavalry Brigade, District of Central and Northern Alabama, Department of Alabama, Mississippi and East Louisiana (February-September 1864)

Artillery, District of Central Alabama, Department of Alabama, Mississippi and East Louisiana (September 1864-March 1865)

Light Artillery, District of the Gulf, Department of Alabama, Mississippi and East Louisiana (one section) (February 1865)

Artillery, District of Alabama, Department of Alabama, Mississippi and East Louisiana (March-April 1865)

Battles: Wilson's Raid (March 22-April 24, 1865)

Columbus, Georgia (detachment) (April 16, 1865)

29. ALABAMA MARKS ARTILLERY BATTERY

Organization: Organized at Montgomery on March 1, 1862. Mustered in on March 7, 1862. Armed with four 12-lb. Napoleons between March 29, 1864, and April 1, 1864. Surrendered at Augusta, Georgia, in April 1865.

First Commander: Henry C. Semple (Captain)

Captain: Richard W. Goldthwaite

Assignments: Army of Mobile, Department of Alabama and West Florida (March-June 1862)

Army of Mobile, District of the Gulf, Department #2 (July 1862)

Wood's Brigade, Buckner's Division, Left Wing, Army of the Mississippi, Department #2 (October-November 1862)

Wood's Brigade, Buckner's-Cleburne's Division, 2nd Corps, Army of Tennessee (November 1862-August 1863)

Artillery Battalion, Cleburne's Division, 2nd Corps, Army of Tennessee (August-November 1863)

Artillery Battalion, Cleburne's Division, 1st Corps, Army of Tennessee (November 1863-February 1864)

Hotchkiss' Battalion, Artillery, 1st Corps, Army of Tennessee (February-December 1864)

District of Georgia, Department of Tennessee and Georgia (presumably) (March-April 1865)

Battles: Perryville (October 8, 1862)

Murfreesboro (December 31, 1862-January 3, 1863)

Tullahoma Campaign (June 1863)

Liberty Gap (June 24, 1863)

Chickamauga (September 19-20, 1863)

Chattanooga Siege (September-November 1863)

Chattanooga (November 23-25, 1863)

Ringgold Gap (November 26, 1864)

Atlanta Campaign (May-September 1864)

Resaca (May 14-15, 1864)

Atlanta (July 22, 1864)

Atlanta Siege (July-September 1864)

Jonesboro (August 31-September 1, 1864)

Franklin (November 30, 1864)

Nashville (December 15-16, 1864)

30. ALABAMA MOHAWK ARTILLERY BATTERY

See: LOUISIANA 12TH HEAVY ARTILLERY BATTALION, COMPANY E

31. ALABAMA MONTGOMERY TRUE BLUES ARTILLERY BATTERY

Organization: Organized by the conversion of 1st Company G, 3rd Infantry Regiment, to artillery service at Norfolk, Virginia, in January 1862. Disbanded at Ridgeway, Warren County, North Carolina, in April 1865.

First Commander: William G. Andrews (Captain)

Captain: Edgar G. Lee

Assignments: Saunders' Artillery Battalion, Department of Norfolk (January 1862)

French's Command, Department of North Carolina and Southern Virginia (September 1862-February 1863)

Reserve Artillery, D. H. Hill's Command, Department of North Carolina and Southern Virginia (February-April 1863)

Artillery, Department of North Carolina (April-July 1863)

Saunders' Artillery Battalion, District of North Carolina, Department of North Carolina and Southern Virginia (July-September 1863)

Saunders' Artillery Battalion, Department of North Carolina (September 1863-May 1864)

Artillery, 2nd Military District, Department of North Carolina and Southern Virginia (May-June 1864)

Moseley's Battalion, Artillery, Department of North Carolina and Southern Virginia (June 1864)

2nd Military District, Department of North Carolina and Southern Virginia (June 1864-January 1865)

3rd Sub-district, 2nd Military District, Department of North Carolina (January-March 1865)

Light Artillery, Department of North Carolina (March-April 1865)

Battle: New Bern (March 14, 1862)

32. ALABAMA (AND FLORIDA) ROBERTSON'S-DENT'S ARTILLERY BATTERY

Organization: Organized by the assignment of men from Alabama and Florida at Pensacola, Florida, on December 21, 1861. Armed with four 12-lb. Napoleons on April 6-7, 1862. Armed with six 12-lb. Napoleons on May 19, 1863. Armed with two 6-lb. Smoothbores and two 12-lb. Napoleons between March 29, 1864, and April 4, 1864. Surrendered by Lieutenant Richard Taylor, commanding the Department of Alabama, Mississippi and East Louisiana, at Citronelle, Alabama, on May 4, 1865.

First Commander: Felix H. Robertson (Captain)

Captain: S. H. Dent

Assignments: Army of Pensacola, Department of Alabama and West Florida (December 1861-January 1862)

Wheeler's Brigade, 2nd Corps, 2nd Grand Division, Army of the Mississippi, Department #2 (March 1862)

Gladden's-Gardner's Brigade, Withers' Division, 2nd Corps, Army of the Mississippi, Department #2 (March-June 1862)

Gardner's Brigade, Reserve Corps, Army of the Mississippi, Department #2 (June-July 1862)

Gardner's Brigade, Reserve Division, Army of the Mississippi, Department #2 (July-August 1862)

Gardner's Brigade, Withers' Division, Right Wing, Army of the Mississippi, Department #2 (August-November 1862)

Gardner's-Loomis'-Coltart's-Deas' Brigade, Withers' Division, 1st Corps, Army of Tennessee (November 1862-March 1863)

Chalmers'-Anderson's Brigade, Withers'-Hindman's Division, 1st Corps, Army of Tennessee (March-August 1863)

Deas' Brigade, Hindman's Division, 1st Corps, Army of Tennessee (September 1863)

Artillery Battalion, Hindman's Division, 1st Corps, Army of Tennessee (October-November 1863)

Artillery Battalion, Hindman's Division, 2nd Corps, Army of Tennessee (November 1863-February 1864)

Courtney's Battalion, Artillery, 2nd Corps, Army of Tennessee (February 1864-January 1865)

Hoxton's Artillery Battalion, Left Wing, Defenses of Mobile, Artillery Reserves, etc., Department of Alabama, Mississippi and East Louisiana (March-April 1865)

Hoxton's Artillery Battalion, Fuller's Regiment, Department of Alabama, Mississippi and East Louisiana (April-May 1865)

Battles: Pensacola (January 1, 1862)

Shiloh (April 6-7, 1862)

Corinth Campaign (April-June 1862)

Farmington (May 1862)

Bridge Creek (May 27, 1862)

Murfreesboro (December 31, 1862-January 3, 1863)

Tullahoma Campaign (June 1863)

Chickamauga (September 19-20, 1863)

Chattanooga Siege (September-November 1863)

Chattanooga (November 23-25, 1863)

Atlanta Campaign (May-September 1864)

Atlanta Siege (July-September 1864)

Franklin (November 30, 1864)

Nashville (December 15-16, 1864)

Mobile (March 17-April 12, 1865)

33. ALABAMA SEAWELL'S ARTILLERY BATTERY
See: LOUISIANA 12TH HEAVY ARTILLERY BATTALION, COMPANY E

34. ALABAMA STATE ARTILLERY BATTERY
Also Known As: Ketchum's-Garrity's Artillery Battery
Organization: Organized at Mobile on May 4, 1865. Armed with four 6-lb. Smoothbores and two 12-lb. Howitzers on April 6-7, 1862. Armed with two 6-lb. Smoothbores and two 12-lb. Howitzers on May 19, 1863. Armed with two 3-inch Rifles and two 10-lb. Parrotts between March 29, 1864, and April 1, 1864. Surrendered by Lieutenant Richard Taylor, commanding the Depart-

ment of Alabama, Mississippi and East Louisiana, at Citronelle, Alabama, on May 4, 1865.

First Commander: William H. Ketchum (Captain)

Captain: James Garrity

Assignments: Army of Pensacola, Department of Alabama and West Florida (October 1861-March 1862)

D. W. Adams' Brigade, 2nd Corps, Army of the Mississippi, Department #2 (March 1862)

Pond's-Ruggles' Brigade, Ruggles' Division, 2nd Corps, Army of the Mississippi, Department #2 (March-June 1862)

Chalmers' Brigade, Reserve Corps, Army of the Mississippi, Department #2 (June-July 1862)

Chalmers' Brigade, Reserve Division, Army of the Mississippi, Department #2 (July-August 1862)

Chalmers' Brigade, Withers' Division, Right Wing, Army of the Mississippi, Department #2 (August-November 1862)

Chalmers' Brigade, Withers' Division, 1st Corps, Army of Tennessee (November 1862-March 1863)

Deas' Brigade, Withers'-Hindman's Division, 1st Corps, Army of Tennessee (March-August 1863)

Anderson's Brigade, Hindman's Division, 1st Corps, Army of Tennessee (September 1863)

Artillery Battalion, Hindman's Division, 1st Corps, Army of Tennessee (October-November 1863)

Artillery Battalion, Hindman's Division, 2nd Corps, Army of Tennessee (November 1863-February 1864)

Courtney's Battalion, Artillery, 2nd Corps, Army of Tennessee (February 1864-January 1865)

Hoxton's Artillery Battalion, Left Wing, Defenses of Mobile, Artillery Reserves, etc., Department of Alabama, Mississippi and East Louisiana (March-April 1865)

Hoxton's Artillery Battalion, Fuller's Brigade, Department of Alabama, Mississippi and East Louisiana (April-May 1865)

Battles: Santa Rosa Island (October 9, 1861)

Expedition toward Purdy and operations about Crump's Landing (March 9-14, 1862)

Shiloh (April 6-7, 1862)

Corinth Campaign (April-June 1862)

Farmington (May 1864)

Munfordville (September 17, 1862)

Wildcat Gap (October 17-20, 1862)

Murfreesboro (December 31, 1862-January 3, 1863)
Tullahoma Campaign (June 1863)
Chickamauga (September 19-20, 1863)
Chattanooga Siege (September-November 1863)
Chattanooga (November 23-25, 1863)
Atlanta Campaign (May-September 1864)
New Hope Church (May 25-June 4, 1864)
Atlanta Siege (July-September 1864)
Jonesboro (August 31-September 1, 1864)
Marietta (June 1864)
Resaca (October 13, 1864)
King's Hill (one section) (October 23, 1864)
Gadsden Road (section) (October 25, 1864)
Columbia (November 29, 1864)
Franklin (November 30, 1864)
Nashville (December 15-16, 1864)
Mobile (March 17-April 12, 1865)
Spanish Fort (April 2-8, 1865)

35. ALABAMA TARRANT'S ARTILLERY BATTERY

Organization: Organized in June 1863. Armed with four 6-lb. Smoothbores on January 11, 1864. Armed with two 12-lb. Howitzers and two 3-inch Rifles on May 19, 1864. Surrendered at Fort Blakely on April 9, 1865. Exchanged at Vicksburg, Warren County, Mississippi, on April 28, 1865. Surrendered by Lieutenant Richard Taylor, commanding the Department of Alabama, Mississippi and East Louisiana, at Citronelle, Alabama, on May 4, 1865.

First Commander: Edward Tarrant (Captain)

Assignments: Eastern Division, Department of the Gulf (September 1863)
Clanton's Brigade, Department of the Gulf (September 1863-January 1864)
Reynolds' Brigade, District of the Gulf, Department of Alabama, Mississippi and East Louisiana (April-May 1864)
Artillery Battalion, Cantey's-Walthall's Division, Army of Mississippi (May-July 1864)
Preston's-Truehart's Battalion, Artillery, 3rd Corps, Army of Tennessee (July 1864-January 1865)
Grayson's Artillery Battalion, Right Wing, Defenses of Mobile, Artillery Reserves, etc., Department of Alabama, Mississippi and East Louisiana (March-April 1865)
Grayson's Artillery Battalion, Smith's Regiment, Department of Alabama, Mississippi and East Louisiana (April-May 1865)

Battles: Atlanta Campaign (May-September 1864)

Cassville (May 19-22, 1864)
New Hope Church (May 25-June 4, 1864)
Lost Mountain (June 10, 1864)
Kennesaw Mountain (June 27, 1864)
Peach Tree Creek (July 20, 1864)
Atlanta (July 22, 1864)
Nashville (December 15-16, 1864)
Mobile (March 17-April 12, 1865)
Fort Blakely (April 1-9, 1865)

36. ALABAMA WADDELL'S ARTILLERY BATTERY

Organization: Organized from reenlisting men of the 6th Infantry Regiment at Davis Ford, Virginia, in February 1862. Regiment surrendered at Vicksburg, Mississippi, on July 4, 1863. Paroled there later in month. Declared exchanged on September 12, 1863. Increased to a battalion and designated as the 20th Light Artillery Battalion in October 1863.

First Commander: James F. Waddell (Captain)

Assignments: Tracy's Brigade, McCown's Division, Department of East Tennessee (October-December 1862)

Tracy's Brigade, Stevenson's Division, 2nd Military District, Department of Mississippi and East Louisiana (January-February 1863)

Artillery Battalion, Stevenson's Division, 2nd Military District, Department of Mississippi and East Louisiana (March-April 1863)

Tracy's-Garrott's-Lee's Brigade, Stevenson's Division, Department of Mississippi and East Louisiana (April-July 1863)

Battles: Richmond, Kentucky (August 29-30, 1862)

Vicksburg Campaign (May-July 1863)

Champion Hill (May 16, 1863)

Vicksburg Siege (May-July 1863)

37. ALABAMA WARD'S-CRUSE'S ARTILLERY BATTERY

Organization: Organized in the fall of 1862. Mustered in at Huntsville on October 10, 1862. Armed with four 12-lb. Napoleons on January 11, 1864. Captured at Selma on April 2, 1865.

First Commander: John J. Ward (Captain)

Captain: Samuel R. Cruse

Assignments: Slaughter's Brigade, Department of the Gulf (June 1863)

Cantey's Brigade, Western Division, Department of the Gulf (August 1863)

Cantey's Brigade, Department of the Gulf (August 1863-January 1864)

Shoup's-Fuller's Artillery Brigade, Department of the Gulf (February-April 1864)

Fuller's Artillery Brigade, District of the Gulf, Department of Alabama, Mississippi and East Louisiana (April-May 1864)
Artillery Battalion, French's Division, Army of Mississippi (May-July 1864)
Storrs' Battalion, Artillery, Army of Mississippi (July 1864)
Storrs' Battalion, Artillery, 3rd Corps, Army of Tennessee (July-September 1864)
Battles: Atlanta Campaign (May-September 1864)
Atlanta Siege (July-September 1864)
Wilson's Raid (March 22-April 24, 1865)
Selma (April 2, 1865)

CAVALRY

38. ALABAMA 1ST CAVALRY BATTALION

See: ALABAMA 12TH CAVALRY BATTALION, PARTISAN RANGERS

39. ALABAMA 1ST CAVALRY BATTALION, PARTISAN RANGERS

Also Known As: Alabama 1st Cavalry Battalion

Organization: Organized with four companies on June 25, 1862. Consolidated into three companies and designated as the 18th Infantry Battalion in late 1862.

First Commander: William T. Gunter (Major)

Assignment: Department of East Tennessee (August-October 1862)

40. ALABAMA 1ST (BEALL'S) CAVALRY BATTALION

Organization: Organized with three companies, one of them from Georgia. Consolidated with the 2nd (Brewer's) Mississippi and Alabama Cavalry Battalion and Company K, 2nd Mississippi Infantry Battalion, and designated as the 8th (Wade's) Confederate Cavalry Regiment in May 1862.

First Commander: Thaddeus S. Beall (Major)

Assignment: Beall's Cavalry Brigade, Department #2 (April-May 1862)

Battle: Corinth Campaign (April-June 1862)

41. ALABAMA 1ST CAVALRY REGIMENT

Organization: Organized at Montgomery ca. November 12, 1861. Reduced to seven companies in November 1862. Companies 2nd H, 2nd I, 2nd K and L assigned from the 12th Partisan Rangers Battalion in November 1862. These four companies detached at some time prior to June 30, 1864, and reformed the 12th Partisan Rangers Battalion. Original companies reconstituted at the same time. Surrendered by General Joseph E. Johnston at Durham Station, Orange County, North Carolina, on April 26, 1865.

First Commander: James H. Clanton (Colonel)

Field Officers: William W. Allen (Major, Lieutenant Colonel, Colonel)
David T. Blakely (Major, Lieutenant Colonel, Colonel)
Thomas B. Brown (Lieutenant Colonel)
Moses W. Hannon (Lieutenant Colonel)
William W. Hundley (Lieutenant Colonel)
Augustus H. Johnson (Major)

Assignments: Walker's Brigade, 1st Corps, 2nd Grand Division, Army of the
Mississippi, Department #2 (March 1862)
Cavalry Brigade, 2nd Grand Division, Army of the Mississippi, Department #2
(March 1862)
Cavalry Brigade, 2nd Corps, Army of the Mississippi, Department #2 (March
1862)
Cavalry, Army of the Mississippi, Department #2 (April 1862)
Beall's Cavalry Brigade, Department #2 (April-June 1862)
Chalmers' Brigade, Withers' Division, 2nd Corps, Army of the Mississippi,
Department #2 (June 1862)
Wheeler's Cavalry Brigade, Left Wing, Army of the Mississippi, Department
#2 (August-September 1862)
Forrest's Cavalry Brigade, Right Wing, Army of the Mississippi, Department
#2 (September 1862)
Wheeler's Cavalry Brigade, Left Wing, Army of the Mississippi, Department
#2 (October-November 1862)
Wheeler's Cavalry Brigade, 2nd Corps, Army of Tennessee (November 1862)
Wheeler's-Hagan's Brigade, Wheeler's Cavalry Division, Army of Tennessee
(December 1862-March 1863)
Hagan's-Morgan's Brigade, Martin's Division, Wheeler's Cavalry Corps, Army
of Tennessee (March-November 1863)
Morgan's-Russell's Brigade, Martin's-Morgan's Division, Martin's Cavalry
Corps, Department of East Tennessee (November 1863-February 1864)
Morgan's-Allen's-Hagan's Brigade, Martin's-Morgan's-Allen's Division,
Wheeler's Cavalry Corps, Army of Tennessee (April-November 1864)
Hagan's Brigade, Allen's Division, Wheeler's Cavalry Corps, Department of
South Carolina, Georgia, and Florida (November 1864-February 1865)
Hagan's Brigade, Allen's Division, Hampton's Cavalry Command (February-
April 1865)
Hagan's Brigade, Allen's Division, Wheeler's Cavalry Corps, Hampton's Cav-
alry Command, Army of Tennessee (April 1865)

Battles: near Monterey, Tennessee (April 3, 1862)
near Pittsburg, Tennessee (April 4, 1862)
Shiloh (April 6-7, 1862)
Munfordville (September 17, 1862)

Woodsonville (September 21, 1862)
Perryville (October 8, 1862)
Nashville (November 5, 1862)
near Lavergne, Tennessee (November 27, 1862)
Stewart's Creek Bridge (December 27, 1862)
Murfreesboro (December 31, 1862-January 3, 1863)
Tullahoma Campaign (June 1863)
Chickamauga (September 19-20, 1863)
Chattanooga Siege (September-November 1863)
Wheeler's Sequatchie Raid (October 1-9, 1863)
Knoxville Siege (November 1863)
Atlanta Campaign (May-September 1864)
Kennesaw Mountain (June 27, 1864)
Big Shanty (June 9, 1864)
Noonday Creek (June 1864)
Atlanta Siege (July-September 1864)
Savannah Campaign (November-December 1864)
Carolinas Campaign (February-April 1865)
Bentonville (March 19-21, 1865)

42. ALABAMA 1ST CAVALRY REGIMENT, PARTISAN RANGERS
See: ALABAMA 51ST CAVALRY REGIMENT, PARTISAN RANGERS

43. ALABAMA 2ND CAVALRY BATTALION
See: ALABAMA 19TH CAVALRY BATTALION

44. ALABAMA 2ND CAVALRY REGIMENT
Organization: Organized and mustered into Confederate service for three years or the war at Montgomery on May 1, 1862. Surrendered as part of Jefferson Davis' escort at Forsyth, Georgia, in May 1865
First Commander: Fountain W. Hunter (Colonel)
Field Officers: John N. Carpenter (Major, Lieutenant Colonel, Colonel)
Richard W. Carter (Major)
James Cunningham (Lieutenant Colonel)
Richard G. Earle (Colonel)
Matthew R. Marks (Major)
Leroy Napier (temporary assignment) (Major)
Josiah J. Pegues (Major, Lieutenant Colonel)
John P. West (Lieutenant Colonel)
Assignments: Detachment of Observation, District of the Gulf, Department
  #2 (October-November 1862)

Eastern Division (Cantey), Department of the Gulf (April-May 1863)

Ferguson's Brigade, Lee's Cavalry Corps, Department of Mississippi and East Louisiana (August-December 1863)

Ferguson's Brigade, Jackson's Division, Lee's Cavalry Corps, Department of Mississippi and East Louisiana (January 1864)

Ferguson's Brigade, Jackson's Division, Lee's Cavalry Corps, Department of Alabama, Mississippi and East Louisiana (January-May 1864)

Ferguson's Brigade, Jackson's Division, Army of Mississippi (May-July 1864)

Ferguson's Brigade, Jackson's Cavalry Division, Army of Tennessee (July-October 1864)

Ferguson's Brigade, Iverson's-Young's Division, Wheeler's Cavalry Corps, Department of South Carolina, Georgia and Florida (December 1864-February 1865)

Ferguson's Brigade, Young's Division, Wheeler's Cavalry Corps, Hampton's Cavalry Command (February-April 1865)

Ferguson's Brigade, Young's Division, Wheeler's Cavalry Corps, Hampton's Cavalry Command, Army of Tennessee (April 1865)

Jefferson Davis' Escort (April-May 1865)

Battles: Russellville (two companies) (July 29, 1862)

Grierson's Raid (April 17-May 2, 1863)

King's Creek (May 5, 1863)

Vincent's Crossroads, near Bay Springs, Mississippi (October 26, 1863)

Atlanta Campaign (May-September 1864)

Atlanta (July 22, 1864)

Atlanta Siege (July-September 1864)

Savannah Campaign (November-December 1864)

Carolinas Campaign (February-April 1865)

45. ALABAMA 3RD CAVALRY REGIMENT

Organization: Organized at Tupelo, Mississippi, on July 1, 1862. Surrendered by General Joseph E. Johnston at Durham Station, Orange County, North Carolina, on April 26, 1865.

First Commander: James Hagan (Colonel)

Field Officers: John D. Farish (Major)

Frank Y. Gaines (Major)

Tyirie A. Mauldin (Lieutenant Colonel)

Josiah Robins (Major)

Assignments: Wheeler's Cavalry Brigade, Left Wing, Army of the Mississippi, Department #2 (October-November 1862)

Wheeler's Cavalry Brigade, 2nd Corps, Army of Tennessee (November-December 1862)

Wheeler's-Hagan's Brigade, Wheeler's Cavalry Division, Army of Tennessee (December 1862-March 1863)

Hagan's-Morgan's Brigade, Martin's Division, Wheeler's Cavalry Corps, Army of Tennessee (March-November 1863)

Morgan's-Russell's Brigade, Martin's-Morgan's Division, Wheeler's Cavalry Corps, Army of Tennessee (November 1863-February 1864)

Morgan's-Allen's-Hagan's Brigade, Martin's-Morgan's-Allen's Division, Wheeler's Cavalry Corps, Army of Tennessee (April-November 1864)

Hagan's Brigade, Allen's Division, Wheeler's Cavalry Corps, Department of South Carolina, Georgia and Florida (November 1864-February 1865)

Hagan's Brigade, Allen's Division, Wheeler's Cavalry Corps, Hampton's Cavalry Command (February-April 1865)

Hagan's Brigade, Allen's Division, Wheeler's Cavalry Corps, Hampton's Cavalry Command, Army of Tennessee (April 1865)

Battles: Perryville (October 8, 1862)
Murfreesboro (December 31, 1862-January 3, 1863)
Tullahoma Campaign (June 1863)
Shelbyville (June 27, 1863)
Chickamauga (September 19-20, 1863)
Wheeler's Sequatchie Raid (October 1-9, 1863)
Knoxville Siege (November 1863)
Russellville (December 10, 1863)
Mossy Creek (December 29, 1863)
Atlanta Campaign (May-September 1864)
Atlanta (July 22, 1864)
Atlanta Siege (July-September 1864)
Savannah Campaign (November-December 1864)
Macon (November 21, 1864)
Carolinas Campaign (February-April 1865)
Aiken (February 11, 1865)
Fayetteville (March 13, 1865)
Bentonville (March 19-21, 1865)
Raleigh (April 12, 1865)
Chapel Hill (April 15, 1865)
Further Reading: Mims, Wilbur F. *War History of the Prattville Dragoons.*

46. ALABAMA 4TH CAVALRY BATTALION

Organization: Organized with three companies from August to September 1863. Field consolidation with Cavalry Battalion, Phillips' Georgia Legion, from May 1864 to July 11, 1864. Merged into the Jeff. Davis Mississippi Cavalry Legion on July 11, 1864. (Order not carried out until November 1864.)

First Commander: Andrew P. Love (Captain and acting major)
Assignment: Young's Brigade, Hampton's-Butler's Division, Cavalry Corps, Army of Northern Virginia (May-November 1864)
Battles: The Wilderness (May 5-6, 1864)
Spotsylvania Court House (May 8-21, 1864)
North Anna (May 23-26, 1864)
Cold Harbor (June 1-3, 1864)
Petersburg Siege (June1864-April 1865)

47.   ALABAMA 4TH (FORREST'S [J. E.]) CAVALRY REGIMENT
See: ALABAMA FORREST'S (J. E.) CAVALRY REGIMENT

48.   ALABAMA 4TH (RODDEY'S) CAVALRY REGIMENT
Organization: Organized at Tuscumbia on October 21, 1862. Mustered into Confederate service on November 1, 1862. Surrendered by Lieutenant Richard Taylor, commanding the Department of Alabama, Mississippi and East Louisiana, at Meridian, Mississippi, on May 4, 1865.
First Commander: Philip D. Roddey (Colonel)
Field Officers: Richard W. Johnson (Major)
William A. Johnson (Major, Lieutenant Colonel, Colonel)
John E. Newsom (Major)
F. M. Windes (Lieutenant Colonel)
Assignments: Roddey's Brigade, Van Dorn's Cavalry Division, Department of Mississippi and East Louisiana (January-February 1863)
Roddey's Brigade, Martin's Division, Van Dorn's Cavalry Corps, Department of Mississippi and East Louisiana (February 1863)
Roddey's Brigade, Wheeler's Cavalry Division, Army of Tennessee (February-March 1863)
Roddey's Brigade, Martin's Division, Wheeler's Cavalry Corps, Army of Tennessee (March 1863)
District of Northern Alabama, Department of Tennessee (March-August 1863)
Roddey's Brigade, Wheeler's Cavalry Corps, Army of Tennessee (August 1863-September 1864)
District of Northern Alabama, Department of Alabama, Mississippi and East Louisiana (September 1864-March 1865)
Roddey's Brigade, Forrest's Cavalry Corps, Department of Alabama, Mississippi and East Louisiana (March-May 1865)
Battles: Cherokee Station and Little Bear Creek, Alabama (December 12, 1862)
Streight's Raid (April-May 1863)

Chickamauga (September 19-20, 1863)
Knoxville Siege (November 1863)
Atlanta Campaign (May-September 1864)
vs. Sturgis' Mississippi Expedition (June 1-13, 1864)
Atlanta Siege (July-September 1864)
Wilson's Raid (March 22-April 24, 1865)
Selma (April 2, 1865)
Further Reading: Wyeth, John Allen. *With Sabre and Scapel, the Autobiography of a Soldier and Surgeon.*

49. ALABAMA 4TH (RUSSELL'S) CAVALRY REGIMENT

Organization: Organized by the consolidation of the 15th Tennessee Cavalry Battalion and four companies of the 3rd Tennessee Cavalry Regiment at Murfreesboro, Tennessee, on November 23, 1862. Field consolidation with the 7th Cavalry Regiment from January 19, 1865, to May 4, 1865. Surrendered at Gainesville, Alabama, on May 4, 1865.

First Commander: Alfred A. Russell (Colonel)

Field Officers: Joseph M. Hambrick (Lieutenant Colonel)
F. M. Taylor (Major)

Assignments: Russell's Brigade, Martin's Division, Wheeler's Cavalry Corps, Army of Tennessee (July-September 1863)

Morgan's Brigade, Martin's Division, Army of Tennessee (October-November 1863)

Morgan's-Russell's Brigade, Martin's-Morgan's Division, Martin's Cavalry Corps, Department of East Tennessee (December 1863-February 1864)

Morgan's-Allen's-Hagan's Brigade, Martin's-Morgan's-Allen's Division, Wheeler's Cavalry Corps, Army of Tennessee (April-November 1864)

District of Northern Alabama, Department of Alabama, Mississippi and East Louisiana (November 1864)

Chalmers' Division, Forrest's Cavalry Corps, Department of Alabama, Mississippi and East Louisiana (January-February 1865)

Buford's Division, Forrest's Cavalry Corps, Department of Alabama, Mississippi and East Louisiana (February-May 1865)

Battles: Forrest's West Tennessee Raid (December 11, 1862-January 3, 1863)
Spring Creek (December 20-21, 1862)
Parker's Crossroads (December 31, 1862)
Unionville, Tennessee (March 4, 1863)
Rover, Tennessee (March 13, 1863)
Tullahoma Campaign (June 1863)
Chickamauga (September 19-20, 1863)
Chattanooga Siege (September-November 1863)

Wheeler's Sequatchie Raid (October 1-9, 1863)
Knoxville Siege (November 1863)
Atlanta Campaign (May-September 1864)
Atlanta Siege (July-September 1864)
Sunshine Church (July 31, 1864)

50. ALABAMA 5TH CAVALRY REGIMENT

Organization: Organized by the increasing of the 22nd Cavalry Battalion to a regiment at Tuscumbia in December 1862. Surrendered by Lieutenant Richard Taylor, commanding the Department of Alabama, Mississippi and East Louisiana, at Meridian, Mississippi, on May 4, 1865.

First Commander: Josiah Patterson (Colonel)

Field Officers: R. F. Gibson (Major)
James M. Warren (Lieutenant Colonel)

Assignments: District of Northern Alabama, Department of Tennessee (May-August 1863)
Roddey's Brigade, Wheeler's Cavalry Corps, Army of Tennessee (August 1863-September 1864)
District of Northern Alabama, Department of Alabama, Mississippi and East Louisiana (September 1864-March 1865)
Roddey's Brigade, Forrest's Cavalry Corps, Department of Alabama, Mississippi and East Louisiana (March-May 1865)

Battles: Cherokee Station and Little Bear Creek, Alabama (December 12, 1862)
Chickamauga (September 19-20, 1863)
Chattanooga Siege (September-November 1863)
Knoxville Siege (November 1863)
Atlanta Campaign (May-September 1864)
Atlanta Siege (July-September 1864)
Forrest's Middle Tennessee Raid (September-October 1864)
Wilson's Raid (March 22-24, 1865)

51. ALABAMA 6TH CAVALRY REGIMENT

Organization: Organized in early 1863. Surrendered by Lieutenant Richard Taylor, commanding the Department of Alabama, Mississippi and East Louisiana, at Meridian, Mississippi, on May 4, 1865.

First Commander: Charles H. Colvin (Colonel)

Field Officers: Washington T. Lary (Lieutenant Colonel)
Eliphalet A. McWhorter (Major)

Assignments: Clanton's Brigade, Western Division, Department of the Gulf (July-August 1863)

Clanton's Brigade, Department of the Gulf (September-December 1863)
Jenifer's Cavalry Brigade, Department of the Gulf (December 1863-February 1864)
Clanton's Brigade, District of Central and Northern Alabama, Department of Alabama, Mississippi and East Louisiana (February-May 1864)
Armstrong's Brigade, Jackson's Cavalry Division, Army of Mississippi (May-September 1864)
Clanton's Brigade, District of Central Alabama, Department of Alabama, Mississippi and East Louisiana (September-December 1864)
Clanton's Brigade, District of the Gulf, Department of Alabama, Mississippi and East Louisiana (February-April 1865)
Clanton's Brigade, Department of Alabama, Mississippi and East Louisiana (April-May 1865)
Battles: Decatur (July 1864)
Atlanta Campaign (May-September 1864)
Atlanta Siege (July-September 1864)
Ten Islands (August 14, 1864)
Mobile (March 17-April 12, 1865)
Wilson's Raid (March 22-April 24, 1865)

52. ALABAMA 7TH CAVALRY REGIMENT

Also Known As: Alabama 6th Cavalry Regiment
Organization: Organized on July 22, 1863. Mustered into Confederate service on July 22, 1863. Field consolidation with the 4th (Roddey's) Cavalry Regiment from January 19, 1865, to May 4, 1865. Surrendered by Lieutenant Richard Taylor, commanding the Department of Alabama, Mississippi and East Louisiana, at Meridian, Mississippi, on May 4, 1865.
First Commander: Joseph Hodgson (Colonel)
Field Officers: Turner Clanton, Jr. (Major, Lieutenant Colonel)
Henry J. Livingston (Lieutenant Colonel)
Francis C. Randolph (Major, Lieutenant Colonel, Colonel)
Assignments: Eastern Division, Department of the Gulf (September 1863)
Clanton's Brigade, Department of the Gulf (September-October 1863)
Quarles' Brigade, Department of the Gulf (December 1863-January 1864)
Reynolds' Brigade, Department of the Gulf (March-April 1864)
Reynolds' Brigade, District of the Gulf, Department of Alabama, Mississippi and East Louisiana (April-May 1864)
Unattached, District of the Gulf, Department of Alabama, Mississippi and East Louisiana (May-July 1864)
Patton's Brigade, District of the Gulf, Department of Alabama, Mississippi and East Louisiana (August 1864)

Thomas' Brigade, District of the Gulf, Department of Alabama, Mississippi and East Louisiana (September 1864)
Bell's Brigade, Buford's Division, Forrest's Cavalry Corps, Department of Alabama, Mississippi and East Louisiana (October-November 1864)
Rucker's Brigade, Chalmers' Division, Forrest's Cavalry Corps, Department of Alabama, Mississippi and East Louisiana (November 1864-January 1865)
District of Northern Alabama, Department of Alabama, Mississippi and East Louisiana (January-March 1865)
Roddey's Brigade, Forrest's Cavalry Corps, Department of Alabama, Mississippi and East Louisiana (March-May 1865)
Battles: Nashville (December 15-16, 1864)
Wilson's Raid (March 22-April 24, 1865)
Columbus (April 16, 1865)

53. ALABAMA 7TH (MALONE'S) CAVALRY REGIMENT
See: ALABAMA 9TH CAVALRY REGIMENT

54. ALABAMA 8TH (BALL'S-HATCH'S) CAVALRY REGIMENT

Also Known As: Alabama 9th (Ball's-Hatch's) Cavalry Regiment

Organization: Organized by the increasing of Hatch's Cavalry Battalion, Local Defense Troops (six months), to a regiment at Newbern on April 26, 1864. Surrendered at Gainesville, Alabama, on May 4, 1865.

First Commander: Elias P. Ball (Colonel)

Field Officers: John L. Chancellor (Lieutenant Colonel)
Lemuel D. Hatch (Major, Lieutenant Colonel, Colonel)
William T. Poe (Major)
Richard H. Redwood (Major)

Assignments: Armistead's Brigade, District of Central and Northern Alabama, Department of Alabama, Mississippi and East Louisiana (August-September 1864)
Armistead's Brigade, District of Central Alabama, Department of Alabama, Mississippi and East Louisiana (September-December 1864)
Armistead's Brigade, District of the Gulf, Department of Alabama, Mississippi and East Louisiana (March-April 1865)
Armistead's Brigade, Department of Alabama, Mississippi and East Louisiana (April-May 1865)

Battles: Lafayette (June 24, 1864)
Ten Islands (August 14, 1864)
Mobile (March 17-April 12, 1865)

55. ALABAMA 8TH (LIVINGSTON'S) CAVALRY REGIMENT

Organization: Organization completed by the increasing of Livingston's Cavalry Battalion to a regiment at Gadsden on October 6, 1864. Surrendered at Gainesville, Alabama, on May 4, 1865.
First Commander: Henry J. Livingston (Colonel)
Field Officers: Thomas L. Faulkner (Lieutenant Colonel)
Sidney A. Moses (Major)
Assignments: Clanton's Brigade, District of Central Alabama, Department of Alabama, Mississippi and East Louisiana (August-December 1864)
Clanton's Brigade, District of the Gulf, Department of Alabama, Mississippi and East Louisiana (February-April 1865)
Clanton's Brigade, Department of Alabama, Mississippi and East Louisiana (April-May 1865)
Battles: Ten Islands (August 14, 1864)
Mobile (March 17-April 12, 1865)
Wilson's Raid (March 22-April 24, 1865)

56. ALABAMA 9TH CAVALRY REGIMENT

Organization: Organized by the consolidation of the 14th Partisan Rangers Battalion and the 19th Cavalry Battalion and designated as the 7th Cavalry Regiment on April 15, 1863, per S.O.#25, Wharton's Division. Organization recognized by the Adjutant and Inspector General's Office and designation changed to 9th Cavalry Regiment on September 5, 1864. Surrendered by General Joseph E. Johnston at Durham Station, Orange County, North Carolina, on April 26, 1865.
First Commander: James C. Malone, Jr. (Colonel)
Field Officers: Eugene F. Falconnet (Major)
Zachariah Thomason (Lieutenant Colonel)
Assignments: Crews' Brigade, Wharton's Division, Wheeler's Cavalry Corps, Army of Tennessee (April-October 1863)
Hagan's-Morgan's Brigade, Martin's Division, Wheeler's Cavalry Corps, Department of East Tennessee (October 1863-February 1864)
Morgan's-Russell's Brigade, Martin's-Morgan's Division, Martin's Cavalry Corps, Army of Tennessee (April-October 1864)
Hagan's Brigade, Allen's Division, Wheeler's Cavalry Corps, Department of South Carolina, Georgia and Florida (October 1864-February 1865)
Hagan's Brigade, Allen's Division, Wheeler's Cavalry Corps, Hampton's Cavalry Command (February-April 1865)
Hagan's Brigade, Allen's Division Wheeler's Cavalry Corps, Hampton's Cavalry Command, Army of Tennessee (April 1865)
Battles: Tullahoma Campaign (June 1863)

near Unionville, Tennessee (June 23, 1863)
Chickamauga (September 19-20, 1863)
Chattanooga Siege (September-November 1863)
Knoxville Siege (November 1863)
Talbott's Station (December 29, 1863)
Atlanta Campaign (May-September 1864)
Noonday Creek (June 21, 1864)
Atlanta Siege (July-September 1864)
Savannah Campaign (November-December 1864)
Carolinas Campaign (February-April 1865)
Bentonville (March 19-21, 1865)

57. ALABAMA 9TH (BALL'S-HATCH'S) CAVALRY REGIMENT
See: ALABAMA 8TH (BALL'S-HATCH'S) CAVALRY REGIMENT

58. ALABAMA 10TH CAVALRY REGIMENT
Organization: Organized by the consolidation of Pickett's and Powell's Cavalry Battalions on January 1, 1864. Surrendered by Lieutenant Richard Taylor, commanding the Department of Alabama, Mississippi and East Louisiana, at Citronelle, Alabama on May 4, 1865.
First Commander: Richard O. Pickett (Colonel)
Field Officers: John R. Powell (Lieutenant Colonel)
W. P. Wrenn (Major)
Assignments: District of Northern Alabama, Department of Tennessee (January 1864)
Roddey's Brigade, Wheeler's Cavalry Corps, Army of Tennessee (January-September 1864)
District of Northern Alabama, Department of Alabama, Mississippi and East Louisiana (September 1864-March 1865)
Roddey's Brigade, Forrest's Cavalry Corps, Department of Alabama, Mississippi and East Louisiana (March-May 1865)
Battles: Pulaski Raid (May 1863)
Tupelo (July 14, 1864)
Wilson's Raid (March 22-April 24, 1865)

59. ALABAMA 10TH (BURTWELL'S) CAVALRY REGIMENT
See: ALABAMA 11TH CAVALRY REGIMENT

60. ALABAMA 11TH CAVALRY BATTALION
See: CONFEDERATE 3RD CAVALRY REGIMENT

61. ALABAMA 11TH CAVALRY REGIMENT

Also Known As: Alabama 10th (Burtwell's) Cavalry Regiment
Organization: Organized by the consolidation of Warren's and Williams' Cavalry Battalions on January 14, 1865. Surrendered by Lieutenant Richard Taylor, commanding the Department of Alabama, Mississippi and East Louisiana, at Citronelle, Alabama, on May 4, 1865.
First Commander: John R. B. Burtwell (Colonel)
Field Officers: John F. Doan (Lieutenant Colonel)
Melville W. Sale (Major)
Assignments: District of Northern Alabama, Department of Alabama, Mississippi and East Louisiana (January-March 1865)
Roddey's Brigade, Forrest's Cavalry Corps, Department of Alabama, Mississippi and East Louisiana (March-May 1865)
Battle: Wilson's Raid (March 22-April 24, 1865)

62. ALABAMA 12TH CAVALRY BATTALION, PARTISAN RANGERS

Also Known As: Alabama 1st Cavalry Battalion
Alabama 12th Cavalry Battalion
Organization: Organized with four companies prior to September 12, 1862. Assigned to the 1st Cavalry Regiment in November 1862. Reconstituted with the original four companies prior to June 30, 1864. Companies E, F and G assigned in 1864. Increased to a regiment and designated as the 12th Cavalry Regiment in January 1865.
First Commander: William H. Hundley (Major, Lieutenant Colonel)
Field Officer: Albert G. Bennett (Major)
Assignments: Wheeler's Cavalry Brigade, 2nd Corps, Army of the Mississippi, Department #2 (November 1862)
Allen's-Hagan's Brigade, Martin's-Allen's Division, Wheeler's Cavalry Corps, Army of Tennessee (June-November 1864)
Hagan's Brigade, Allen's Division, Wheeler's Cavalry Corps, Department of South Carolina, Georgia and Florida (November 1864-January 1865)
Battles: Atlanta Campaign (May-September 1864)
Rome (May 17, 1864)
Atlanta (July 22, 1864)
Atlanta Siege (July-September 1864)
Campbellton (July 1864)
Sunshine Church (July 31, 1864)
Savannah Campaign (November-December 1864)
Carolinas Campaign (February-April 1865)

63. ALABAMA 12TH CAVALRY REGIMENT

Organization: Organized by the increasing of the 12th Cavalry Battalion to a regiment in January 1865. Surrendered by General Joseph E. Johnston at Durham Station, Orange County, North Carolina, on April 26, 1865.

First Commander: Wren S. Reese (Colonel)

Field Officers: Augustus J. Ingram (Major)

Marcellus Pointer (Lieutenant Colonel)

Assignments: Hagan's Brigade, Allen's Division, Wheeler's Cavalry Corps, Department of South Carolina, Georgia and Florida (January-February 1865)

Hagan's Brigade, Allen's Division, Wheeler's Cavalry Corps, Hampton's Cavalry Command (February-April 1865)

Hagan's Brigade, Allen's Division, Wheeler's Cavalry Corps, Hampton's Cavalry Command, Army of Tennessee (April 1865)

Battles: Carolinas Campaign (February-April 1865)

Williston, South Carolina (February 8, 1865)

Fayetteville (March 13, 1865)

Averasboro (March 16, 1865)

Bentonville (March 19-21, 1865)

Further Reading: Hendricks, Thomas Wayman. *Cherished Letters of Thomas Wayman Hendricks.*

64. ALABAMA 13TH CAVALRY BATTALION, PARTISAN RANGERS

Organization: Organized with six companies on August 28, 1862. Consolidated with the 15th Partisan Rangers Battalion and designated as the 56th Partisan Rangers Regiment on June 8, 1863.

First Commander: William A. Hewlett (Major)

Assignment: 1st Military District, Department of Mississippi and East Louisiana (December 1862-June 1863)

Battle: King's Creek (May 5, 1863)

65. ALABAMA 14TH CAVALRY BATTALION, PARTISAN RANGERS

Also Known As: 14th Cavalry Battalion

Organization: Organized with six companies prior to December 31, 1862. Consolidated with the 19th Cavalry Battalion and designated as the 7th (later the 9th) Cavalry Regiment on April 15, 1863, per S.O. #25, Wharton's Division.

First Commander: John C. Malone, Jr. (Lieutenant Colonel)

Field Officer: Eugene F. Falconnet (Major)

Assignments: Wharton's Brigade, Wheeler's Cavalry Division, Army of Tennessee (December 1862-March 1863)

Crews' Brigade, Wharton's Division, Wheeler's Cavalry Corps, Army of Tennessee (March-April 1863)
Battles: Murfreesboro (December 31, 1862-January 3, 1863)
Bradyville, Tennessee (March 10, 1863)
Milton, Tennessee (March 20, 1863)

66. ALABAMA 15TH CAVALRY BATTALION, PARTISAN RANGERS

Organization: Organized with five companies on August 25, 1862. Consolidated with the 13th Partisan Rangers Battalion and designated as the 56th Partisan Rangers Regiment on June 8, 1863.
First Commander: William Boyles (Major)
Assignments: Army of Mobile, District of the Gulf, Department #2 (October-November 1862)
Cumming's Brigade, Western Division (Mackall), Department of the Gulf (April-May 1863)
Battle: King's Creek (May 5, 1863)

67. ALABAMA 19TH CAVALRY BATTALION

Also Known As: Alabama 2nd Cavalry Battalion
Organization: Organized with six companies prior to March 30, 1863. Consolidated with the 14th Partisan Rangers Battalion and designated as the 7th (later the 9th) Cavalry Regiment on April 15, 1863, per S.O. #25, Wharton's Division.
First Commander: Zachariah Thomason (Lieutenant Colonel)
Field Officer: Allen Lea (Major)
Assignment: Crews' Brigade, Wharton's Division, Wheeler's Cavalry Corps, Army of Tennessee (March-April 1863)

68. ALABAMA 22ND CAVALRY BATTALION

Organization: Organized with six companies in the summer of 1862. Mustered in for three years on September 1, 1862. Increased to a regiment and designated as the 5th Cavalry Regiment at Tuscumbia in December 1862.
First Commander: James M. Warren (Major)
Battles: near Cherokee, Alabama (December 12, 1862)
Cherokee Station and Little Bear Creek, Alabama (December 12, 1862)

69. ALABAMA 24TH CAVALRY BATTALION

Organization: Organized with three companies on December 31, 1863. Surrendered by General Joseph E. Johnston at Durham Station, Orange County, North Carolina, on April 26, 1865.
First Commander: Robert B. Snodgrass (Major)

Assignments: Roddey's Brigade, Wheeler's Cavalry Corps, Army of Tennessee (December 1863-April 1864)

Hannon's Brigade, Kelly's Division, Wheeler's Cavalry Corps, Army of Tennessee (April-November 1864)

Hannon's Brigade, Iverson's Division, Wheeler's Cavalry Corps, Department of South Carolina, Georgia and Florida (November 1864-January 1865)

Hagan's Brigade, Allen's Division, Wheeler's Cavalry Corps, Department of South Carolina, Georgia and Florida (January-February 1865)

Hagan's Brigade, Allen's Division, Wheeler's Cavalry Corps, Hampton's Cavalry Command (February-April 1865)

Hagan's Brigade, Allen's Division, Wheeler's Cavalry Corps, Hampton's Cavalry Command, Army of Tennessee (April 1865)

Battles: Atlanta Campaign (May-September 1864)

Resaca (May 14-15, 1864)

Atlanta Siege (July-September 1864)

Savannah Campaign (November-December 1864)

Carolinas Campaign (February-April 1865)

70. ALABAMA 25TH CAVALRY BATTALION

Organization: Organized by the assignment of the six Alabama companies of Mead's Confederate Cavalry Regiment on March 2, 1865, per S.O. #52, Adjutant and Inspector General's Office. Final disposition unknown.

First Commander: Miles E. Johnston (Lieutenant Colonel)

Field Officer: Eugene C. Gordon (Major)

Assignment: Duty in Middle Tennessee and northern Alabama (March-May 1865)

71. ALABAMA 51ST CAVALRY REGIMENT, PARTISAN RANGERS

Also Known As: Alabama 1st Cavalry Regiment Partisan Rangers

51st Cavalry Regiment

Organization: Organized on September 2, 1862. Surrendered by General Joseph E. Johnston at Durham Station, Orange County, North Carolina, on April 26, 1865.

First Commander: John T. Morgan (Colonel)

Field Officers: James T. Dye (Major)

Milton L. Kirkpatrick (Lieutenant Colonel, Colonel)

Henry B. Thompson (Major)

James D. Webb (Lieutenant Colonel)

Assignments: Forrest's Cavalry Brigade, Army of Middle Tennessee, Department #2 (October-November 1862)

Forrest's Cavalry Brigade, Army of Tennessee (November 1862)

Wheeler's Brigade, Wheeler's Cavalry Division, Army of Tennessee (December 1862-March 1863)

Hagan's-Morgan's Brigade, Martin's Division, Wheeler's Cavalry Corps, Army of Tennessee (March-November 1863)

Morgan's Brigade, Martin's Division, Martin's Cavalry Corps, Department of East Tennessee (November 1863-February 1864)

Morgan's-Allen's Brigade, Martin's Division, Wheeler's Cavalry Corps, Army of Tennessee (February-November 1864)

Allen's-Hagan's Brigade, Martin's-Allen's Division, Wheeler's Cavalry Corps, Department of South Carolina, Georgia and Florida (November 1864-February 1865)

Hagan's Brigade, Allen's Division, Wheeler's Cavalry Corps, Hampton's Cavalry Command (February-April 1865)

Hagan's Brigade, Allen's Division, Wheeler's Cavalry Corps, Hampton's Cavalry Command, Army of Tennessee (April 1865)

Battles: Lavergne, Tennessee (December 1862)

Murfreesboro (December 31, 1862-January 3, 1863)

Middleton, Unionville, and Rover (January 31, 1863)

Christiana, Tennessee (March 6, 1863)

Tullahoma Campaign (June 1863)

near Decherd (June 29, 1863)

Chickamauga (September 19-20, 1863)

Chattanooga Siege (September-November 1863)

Wheeler's Sequatchie Raid (October 1-9, 1863)

Knoxville Siege (November 1863)

Atlanta Campaign (May-September 1864)

Atlanta (July 22, 1864)

Atlanta Siege (July-September 1864)

Jonesboro (August 31-September 1, 1864)

Savannah Campaign (November-December 1864)

Carolinas Campaign (February-April 1865)

Bentonville (March 19-21, 1865)

72. ALABAMA 53RD CAVALRY REGIMENT, PARTISAN RANGERS

Also Known As: 53rd Cavalry Regiment

Organization: Organized by the increasing of the 1st Cavalry Battalion to a regiment on November 5, 1862. Surrendered by General Joseph E. Johnston at Durham Station, Orange County, North Carolina, on April 26, 1865.

First Commander: Moses W. Hannon (Colonel)

Field Officers: John F. Gaines (Lieutenant Colonel)
Thomas F. Jenkins (Major)

Assignments: District of the Gulf, Department #2 (December 1862)
Armstrong's Brigade, Jackson's Division, Van Dorn's Cavalry Corps, Department of Mississippi and East Louisiana (February 1863)
Armstrong's Brigade, Van Dorn's Cavalry Division, Army of Tennessee (February-March 1863)
Armstrong's Brigade, Jackson's Division, Van Dorn's Cavalry Corps, Army of Tennessee (March 1863)
District of Northern Alabama, Department #2 (July-August 1863)
Roddey's Brigade, Wheeler's Cavalry Corps, Army of Tennessee (August 1863-April 1864)
Hannon's Brigade, Humes' Division, Wheeler's Cavalry Corps, Army of Tennessee (April-November 1864)
Hannon's Brigade, Humes' Division, Wheeler's Cavalry Corps, Department of South Carolina, Georgia and Florida (November 1864-January 1865)
Hannon's Brigade, Allen's Division, Wheeler's Cavalry Corps, Department of South Carolina, Georgia and Florida (January-February 1865)
Hagan's Brigade, Allen's Division, Wheeler's Cavalry Corps, Hampton's Cavalry Command (February-April 1865)
Hagan's Brigade, Allen's Division, Wheeler's Cavalry Corps, Hampton's Cavalry Command, Army of Tennessee (April 1865)

Battles: Cherokee Station and Little Bear Creek, Alabama (December 12, 1862)
Thompson's Station (March 5, 1863)
Florence, Alabama (March 25, 1863)
Brentwood (March 25, 1863)
Town Creek (April 1863)
Streight's Raid (April-May 1863)
Chickamauga (September 19-20, 1863)
Chattanooga Siege (September-November 1863)
Atlanta Campaign (May-September 1864)
Resaca (May 14-15, 1864)
Atlanta Siege (July-September 1864)
Jonesboro (August 31-September 1, 1864)
Carolinas Campaign (February-April 1865)

73. ALABAMA 56TH CAVALRY REGIMENT, PARTISAN RANGERS

Also Known As: 56th Cavalry Regiment

Organization: Organized by the consolidation of the 13th and 15th Partisan Rangers Battalions on June 9, 1863. Surrendered by General Joseph E. Johnston at Durham Station, Orange County, North Carolina, on April 26, 1865.

First Commander: William Boyles (Colonel)

Field Officers: Arthur W. DeBardeleban (Major, Lieutenant Colonel) William A. Hewlett (Lieutenant Colonel) William Martin (Major)

Assignments: Ferguson's Cavalry Brigade, Department of Mississippi and East Louisiana (August 1863)
Ferguson's Brigade, Lee's Cavalry Corps, Department of Mississippi and East Louisiana (November-December 1863)
Ferguson's Brigade, Jackson's Division, Lee's Cavalry Corps, Department of Mississippi and East Louisiana (January 1864)
Ferguson's Brigade, Jackson's Division, Lee's Cavalry Corps, Department of Alabama, Mississippi and East Louisiana (January-May 1864)
Ferguson's Brigade, Jackson's Cavalry Division, Army of Mississippi (May-July 1864)
Ferguson's Brigade, Jackson's Cavalry Division, Army of Tennessee (July-October 1864)
Ferguson's Brigade, Iverson's-Young's Division, Wheeler's Cavalry Corps, Department of South Carolina, Georgia and Florida (December 1864-February 1865)
Ferguson's Brigade, Young's Division, Hampton's Cavalry Command (February-April 1865)
Ferguson's Brigade, Young's Division, Hampton's Cavalry Command, Army of Tennessee (April 1865)

Battles: Atlanta Campaign (May-September 1864)
Atlanta (July 22, 1864)
Atlanta Siege (July-September 1864)
Savannah Campaign (November-December 1864)
Carolinas Campaign (February-April 1865)

74. ALABAMA BARBIERE'S CAVALRY BATTALION, LOCAL DEFENSE TROOPS

Organization: Organized from independent companies of the supporting force for the Conscript Bureau in 1864. Surrendered by Lieutenant Richard Taylor, commanding the Department of Alabama, Mississippi and East Louisiana, at Citronelle, Alabama, on May 4, 1865.

First Commander: Joseph Barbiere (Major)

Assignments: Armistead's Cavalry Brigade, District of Central Alabama, Department of Alabama, Mississippi and East Louisiana (November 1864-January 1865)

District of Central Alabama, Department of Alabama, Mississippi and East Louisiana (April-May 1865)

75. ALABAMA BREWER'S CAVALRY BATTALION

See: MISSISSIPPI AND (ALABAMA) 2ND (BREWER'S) CAVALRY BATTALION

76. ALABAMA FORREST'S (J. E.) CAVALRY REGIMENT

Also Known As: 4th (Forrest's [J. E.]) Cavalry Regiment

Organization: Organized by the increasing of Julian's Cavalry Battalion to a regiment ca. June 1, 1863. Broken up with four Tennessee companies transferred to the 18th Tennessee Cavalry Regiment, four Alabama cavalry companies transferred to Warren's Cavalry Battalion and one Alabama company transferred to Moreland's Cavalry Battalion on July 11, 1864.

First Commander: Jeffrey E. Forrest (Colonel)

Field Officer: Dew M. Wisdom (Lieutenant Colonel)

Assignments: District of Northern Alabama, Department of Tennessee (June-August 1863)

Roddey's Brigade, Wheeler's Cavalry Corps, Army of Tennessee (August-September 1863)

District of Northern Alabama, Department of Tennessee (October-November 1863)

Forrest's Cavalry Corps, Department of Mississippi and East Louisiana (November 1863-January 1864)

J. E. Forrest's Brigade, Chalmers' Division, Forrest's Cavalry Corps, Department of Mississippi and East Louisiana (January 1864)

J. E. Forrest's Brigade, Chalmers' Division, Forrest's Cavalry Corps, Department of Alabama, Mississippi and East Louisiana (January-February 1864)

Thompson's-Crossland's Brigade, Buford's Division, Forrest's Cavalry Corps, Department of Alabama, Mississippi and East Louisiana (February-July 1864)

Battles: Chickamauga (September 19-20, 1863)

Chattanooga Siege (September-November 1863)

Brice's Crossroads (June 10, 1864)

77. ALABAMA HARDIE'S CAVALRY BATTALION RESERVES

Organization: Organized with five companies on September 7, 1864. Surrendered by Lieutenant Richard Taylor, commanding the Department of Alabama, Mississippi and East Louisiana, at Citronelle, Alabama, on May 4, 1865.

First Commander: Joseph Hardie (Major)
Assignments: Armistead's Cavalry Brigade, District of Central Alabama, Department of Alabama, Mississippi and East Louisiana (November 1864- January 1865)
District of Central Alabama, Department of Alabama, Mississippi and East Louisiana (May 1865)

78. ALABAMA HATCH'S CAVALRY BATTALION, LOCAL DEFENSE TROOPS

Organization: Organized with three companies for six months in early 1864. Increased to a regiment and designated as the 8th (Ball's-Hatch's) Cavalry Regiment at Newbern on April 26, 1864.
First Commander: Lemuel D. Hatch (Major)

79. ALABAMA JEFF. DAVIS CAVALRY LEGION

See: MISSISSIPPI JEFF. DAVIS LEGION (COMPOSED OF ALABAMA, GEORGIA AND MISSISSIPPI COMPANIES)

80. ALABAMA JULIAN'S CAVALRY BATTALION

Organization: Organized in early 1863. Increased to a regiment and designated as J. E. Forrest's Cavalry Regiment ca. June 1, 1863.
First Commander: William R. Julian (Lieutenant Colonel)
Field Officer: Dew M. Wisdom (Major)

81. ALABAMA LEWIS' CAVALRY SQUADRON

Organization: Organized with two companies on January 21, 1863. Increased to a battalion and designated as Lewis'-Harrell's Cavalry Battalion on April 26, 1864.
First Commander: Thomas H. Lewis (Captain)

82. ALABAMA LEWIS'-HARRELL'S CAVALRY BATTALION

Organization: Organized with five companies by the increasing of Lewis' Cavalry Squadron to a battalion on April 26, 1864. Surrendered by Lieutenant Richard Taylor, commanding the Department of Alabama, Mississippi and East Louisiana, at Citronelle, Alabama, on May 4, 1865.
First Commander: Thomas H. Lewis (Major)
Field Officer: William V. Harrell (Major)
Assignments: Armistead's Cavalry Brigade, District of Central and North Alabama, Department of Alabama, Mississippi and East Louisiana (August-September 1864)

Armistead's Cavalry Brigade, District of Central Alabama, Department of Alabama, Mississippi and East Louisiana (September-December 1864)

Armistead's Cavalry Brigade, District of the Gulf, Department of Alabama, Mississippi and East Louisiana (March-April 1865)

Armistead's Cavalry Brigade, Department of Alabama, Mississippi and East Louisiana (April-May 1865)

Battles: Lafayette (June 24, 1864)

Mobile (March 17-April 12, 1865)

83. ALABAMA MORELAND'S CAVALRY BATTALION

Organization: Organized with seven companies on August 1, 1863. Company I organized on January 30, 1864. Company H organized on February 1, 1864. Increased to a regiment and designated as Moreland's Cavalry Regiment prior to June 10, 1864.

First Commander: M. D. Moreland (Major, Lieutenant Colonel)

Assignments: District of Northern Alabama, Department of Tennessee (August-September 1863)

Roddey's Brigade, Wheeler's Cavalry Corps, Army of Tennessee (October 1863-February 1864)

District of Northern Alabama, Department of Alabama, Mississippi and East Louisiana (March 1864)

84. ALABAMA MORELAND'S CAVALRY REGIMENT

Organization: Organized by the increasing of Moreland's Cavalry Battalion to a regiment prior to June 10, 1864. Surrendered by Lieutenant Richard Taylor, commanding the Department of Alabama, Mississippi and East Louisiana, at Citronelle, Alabama, on May 4, 1865.

First Commander: M. D. Moreland (Colonel)

Field Officer: J. N. George (Major)

Assignments: Johnson's Brigade, Roddey's Cavalry Division, Department of Alabama, Mississippi and East Louisiana (June-July 1864)

District of North Alabama, Department of Alabama, Mississippi and East Louisiana (September 1864-March 1865)

Roddey's Brigade, Forrest's Cavalry Corps, Department of Alabama, Mississippi and East Louisiana (March-May 1865)

Battles: vs. Sturgis' Mississippi Expedition (June 1-13, 1864)

Brice's Crossroads (June 10, 1864)

Tupelo (July 14, 1864)

Wilson's Raid (March 22-24, 1865)

85. ALABAMA (AND FLORIDA) MURPHY'S CAVALRY BATTALION

Organization: Organized with four companies on June 8, 1863. Increased to a regiment and designated as the 15th Confederate Cavalry Regiment on September 24, 1863.
First Commander: Samuel J. Murphy (Lieutenant Colonel)
Assignment: Department of the Gulf (June-September 1863)

86. ALABAMA MUSGROVE'S CAVALRY BATTALION

Organization: Not listed at the National Archives or in the *Official Records.*
First Commander: Francis A. Musgrove (Major)

87. ALABAMA PICKETT'S CAVALRY BATTALION

Organization: Organized with six companies in August or September 1863. Consolidated with Powell's Cavalry Battalion and designated as the 10th Cavalry Regiment on January 1, 1864.
First Commander: Richard O. Pickett (Major)

88. ALABAMA POWELL'S CAVALRY BATTALION

Organization: Organized with four companies in October or November 1863. Consolidated with Pickett's Cavalry Battalion and designated as the 10th Cavalry Regiment on January 1, 1864.
First Commander: John R. Powell (Major)

89. ALABAMA STUART'S CAVALRY BATTALION

Organization: Organized in early 1864. Not listed at the National Archives. Surrendered by Lieutenant Richard Taylor, commanding the Department of Alabama, Mississippi and East Louisiana, at Citronelle, Alabama, on May 4, 1865.
First Commander: James H. Stuart (Major)
Assignments: District of Northern Alabama, Department of Alabama, Mississippi and East Louisiana (June 1864-February 1865)
Roddey's Brigade, Cavalry Corps, Department of Alabama, Mississippi and East Louisiana (March-May 1865)
Battle: Wilson's Raid (March 22-April 24, 1865)

90. ALABAMA THOMAS' CAVALRY REGIMENT RESERVES

Organization: Organized probably in 1864. Disposition unknown.
First Commander: Bryan M. Thomas (Colonel)
Field Officers: Daniel E. Huger (Lieutenant Colonel)
Lewis (Major)

91. ALABAMA WARREN'S CAVALRY BATTALION

Organization: Organized with four companies ca. July 11, 1864. Consolidated with Williams' Cavalry Battalion and designated as the 11th Cavalry Regiment on January 14, 1865.

First Commander: William H. Warren (Captain)

Assignment: District of Alabama, Department of Alabama, Mississippi and East Louisiana (September-January 1865)

Battle: vs. Sturgis' Mississippi Expedition (June 1-13, 1864)

92. ALABAMA WILLIAMS' CAVALRY BATTALION

Organization: Organized with six companies in 1864. Consolidated with Warren's Cavalry Battalion and designated as the 11th Cavalry Regiment on January 14, 1865.

First Commander: J. T. Williams (Major)

Assignments: Johnson's Brigade, Roddey's Division, Department of Alabama, Mississippi and East Louisiana (July 1864)

District of Northern Alabama, Department of Alabama, Mississippi and East Louisiana (September 1864-January 1865)

Battles: vs. Sturgis' Mississippi Expedition (June 1-13, 1864)

Tupelo (July 14, 1864)

INFANTRY

93. ALABAMA 1ST (LOOMIS') INFANTRY BATTALION
Organization: Organized with five companies on September 17, 1861. Consolidated with the 6th (McClellan's) Infantry Battalion and designated as the 25th Infantry Regiment at Mobile on January 8, 1862.
First Commander: John Q. Loomis (Lieutenant Colonel)
Assignment: District of Alabama, Department of Alabama and West Florida (October 1861-January 1862)

94. ALABAMA 1ST INFANTRY BATTALION RESERVES
Organization: Organized with eight companies in August 1864. Increased to a regiment and designated as the 4th Infantry Regiment Reserves in October 1864.
First Commander: William M. Stone (Lieutenant Colonel)
Assignment: Thomas' Brigade, District of the Gulf, Department of Alabama, Mississippi and East Louisiana (August-October 1864)

95. ALABAMA 1ST INFANTRY REGIMENT
Organization: Organized at Pensacola, Florida, on April 1, 1861. Reorganized at Memphis, Tennessee, on April 2, 1862. Surrendered at Island #10 on April 7, 1862. Exchanged in September 1862. Surrendered at Port Hudson, Louisiana, on July 8, 1863. Enlisted men paroled in July 1863. Officers confined until end of the war. Enlisted men declared exchanged in late 1863. Apparently consolidated with the 16th, 33rd and 45th Infantry Regiments at Smithfield, North Carolina, on April 8, 1865.
First Commander: Henry D. Clayton (Colonel)
Field Officers: Samuel L. Knox (Major)
Michael B. Locke (Lieutenant Colonel)

Iasiah G. W. Steedman (Lieutenant Colonel, Colonel)
Jeremiah N. Williams (Major)

Assignments: Troops at Pensacola (Bragg) (April-October 1861)
Department of Alabama and West Florida (October 1861)
Army of Pensacola, Department of Alabama and West Florida (October 1861-March 1862)
McCown's Command, 1st Geographical Division, Department #2 (March-April 1862)
Fort Pillow, Department #2 (detachment) (April-June 1862)
Grenada, Mississippi, Department #2 (detachment) (June 1862)
3rd Sub-district, District of the Mississippi, Department #2 (July-October 1862)
Heavy Artillery Brigade, 3rd Military District, Department of Mississippi and East Louisiana (October 1862-July 1863)
Unattached, Department of Mississippi and East Louisiana (January 1864)
Quarles' Brigade, Walthall's Division, Army of Mississippi (May-July 1864)
Quarles' Brigade, Walthall's Division, 3rd Corps, Army of Tennessee (July 1864-April 1865)

Battles: Pensacola (April 1861)
Santa Rosa Island (detachment) (October 9, 1861)
Pensacola (November 22-23, 1861)
Island #10 (April 6-7, 1862)
Corinth Campaign (detachment) (April-June 1862)
Port Hudson Bombardment (March 14, 1863)
Port Hudson Siege (May-July 1863)
Atlanta Campaign (May-September 1864)
New Hope Church (May 25-June 4, 1864)
Kennesaw Mountain (June 27, 1864)
Peach Tree Creek (July 20, 1864)
Atlanta (July 22, 1864)
Ezra Church (July 28, 1864)
Atlanta Siege (July-September 1864)
Jonesboro (August 31-September 1, 1864)
Franklin (November 30, 1864)
Nashville (December 15-16, 1864)
Carolinas Campaign (February-April 1865)
Averasboro (March 16, 1865)
Bentonville (March 19-21, 1865)

Further Reading: Barbiere, Joseph. *Scraps from the Prison Table at Camp Chase, and Johnson's Island.* McMorries, Edward Young. *History of the First Alabama Volunteer Infantry, C.S.A.* Smith, Daniel P. *Company K, First Alabama Regiment or Three Years in the Confederate Service.*

96. ALABAMA 1ST INFANTRY REGIMENT CONSOLIDATED

Organization: Organized by the consolidation of the 1st (apparently), 16th, 33rd and 45th Infantry Regiments at Smithfield, North Carolina, on April 8, 1865. 26th Infantry Regiment added to the consolidation in April 1865. 33rd Infantry Regiment transferred to the 17th Infantry Regiment Consolidated, as Companies B, D and F, on April 20, 1865.

First Commander: Robert H. Abercrombie (Colonel)

Assignment: Shelley's Brigade, Loring's Division, 3rd Corps, Army of Tennessee (April 1865)

Battle: Carolinas Campaign (February-April 1865)

97. ALABAMA 1ST INFANTRY REGIMENT RESERVES

Organization: Organized by the increase of Lockhart's Infantry Battalion Reserves in August 1864. Designated as the 62nd Infantry Regiment in the spring of 1865.

First Commander: Daniel E. Huger (Colonel)

Field Officers: James L. Davidson (Lieutenant Colonel)
Bruno F. Yniestra (Major)

Assignments: Liddell's Brigade, District of the Gulf, Department of Alabama, Mississippi and East Louisiana (September 1864)

Withers' Brigade, District of the Gulf, Department of Alabama, Mississippi and East Louisiana (September-October 1864)

Thomas' Brigade, Liddell's Division, District of the Gulf, Department of Alabama, Mississippi and East Louisiana (October-November 1864)

Thomas' Brigade, District of the Gulf, Department of Alabama, Mississippi and East Louisiana (November 1864-March 1865)

Battles: Fort Gaines (August 3-8, 1864)
Mobile (March 17-April 12, 1865)

98. ALABAMA 1ST MOBILE INFANTRY REGIMENT, LOCAL DEFENSE TROOPS

Organization: Organized at Mobile ca. August 23, 1863. Disbanded in April 1865.

First Commander: Alexander W. Lampkin (Colonel)

Field Officers: Stewart W. Cayce (Lieutenant Colonel)
William Hartwell (Major)

Assignments: Cantey's Brigade, Department of the Gulf (December 1863-April 1864)

Cantey's Brigade, District of the Gulf, Department of Alabama, Mississippi and East Louisiana (April 1864)

Unattached, District of the Gulf, Department of Alabama, Mississippi and East
  Louisiana (April-May 1864)
Higgins' Brigade, District of the Gulf, Department of Alabama, Mississippi and
  East Louisiana (June-August 1864)
———— District of the Gulf, Department of Alabama, Mississippi and East
  Louisiana (September 1864)
Taylor's Command, District of the Gulf, Department of Alabama, Mississippi
  and East Louisiana (November 1864-April 1865)
Battle: Mobile (March 17-April 12, 1865)

99. ALABAMA 2ND INFANTRY BATTALION

Also Known As: 1st Infantry Battalion
5th Infantry Battalion
8th Infantry Battalion
Organization: Organized with seven companies on October 29, 1861. In-
creased to a regiment and designated as the 26th (Coltart's) Infantry Regiment
on April 3, 1862.
First Commander: Nicholas Davis (Lieutenant Colonel)
Field Officer: William D. Chadwick (Major, Lieutenant Colonel)
Assignment: Army of Mobile, Department of Alabama and West Florida
(January-February 1862)

100. ALABAMA 2ND INFANTRY REGIMENT

Organization: Organized in April 1861. Disbanded in May 1862.
First Commander: Henry Maury (Colonel)
Field Officers: Henry C. Bradford (Lieutenant Colonel)
Daniel P. Forney (Major)
Assignments: Fort Morgan, Department #2 (May-October 1861)
  District of Alabama, Department of Alabama and West Florida (October
  1861-January 1862)
Army of Mobile, Department of Alabama and West Florida (January-March
  1862)
Fort Pillow, Department #2 (March-May 1862)

101. ALABAMA 2ND INFANTRY REGIMENT MILITIA

Organization: Mustered in with six companies on March 4, 1862. Mustered
out on May 4, 1862.
First Commander: John H. Higley (Colonel)
Field Officers: Alexander W. Lampkin (Major)
Job P. Pillans (Lieutenant Colonel)

102. ALABAMA 2ND INFANTRY REGIMENT RESERVES

Organization: Organized on August 16, 1864. Redesignated as the 63rd Infantry Regiment in March 1865.
First Commander: Olin F. Rice (Colonel)
Field Officers: John H. Echols (Major)
Junius A. Law (Lieutenant Colonel)
Assignments: Liddell's Brigade, District of the Gulf, Department of Alabama, Mississippi and East Louisiana (September 1864)
Withers' Brigade, District of the Gulf, Department of Alabama, Mississippi and East Louisiana (September-October 1864)
Fuller's Brigade, District of the Gulf, Department of Alabama, Mississippi and East Louisiana (October-December 1864)
Thomas' Brigade, District of the Gulf, Department of Alabama, Mississippi and East Louisiana (January-March 1865)
Battle: Mobile (March 17-April 12, 1865)

103. ALABAMA 3RD (COLTART'S) INFANTRY BATTALION

Organization: Organized with eight companies on April 2, 1861. Increased to a regiment and designated as the 7th Infantry Regiment on May 18, 1861.
First Commander: John G. Coltart (Lieutenant Colonel)
Assignment: Pensacola, Florida (April-May 1861)

104. ALABAMA 3RD (SMITH'S) INFANTRY BATTALION

Organization: Organized with nine companies in March 1861. Two companies surrendered at Fort Donelson on February 16, 1862. Increased to a regiment and designated as the 26th Infantry Regiment on March 27, 1862.
First Commander: William R. Smith (Lieutenant Colonel)
Field Officer: John S. Garvin (Major)
Assignments: Drake's Brigade, Fort Henry, Department #2 (two companies) (February 1862)
Drake's Brigade, Johnson's Division, Fort Donelson, Department #2 (two companies) (February 1862)
Battles: Fort Henry (two companies) (February 6, 1862)
Fort Donelson (two companies) (February 12-16, 1862)

105. ALABAMA 3RD INFANTRY BATTALION RESERVES

Organization: Organized in August 1864. Consolidated with the 4th Infantry Battalion Reserves and designated as the 65th Infantry Regiment in March 1865.
First Commander: E. M. Underhill (Lieutenant Colonel)
Field Officer: E. T. Starke (Major)

Assignments: Liddell's Brigade, District of the Gulf, Department of Alabama, Mississippi and East Louisiana (September 1864)

Withers' Brigade, District of the Gulf, Department of Alabama, Mississippi and East Louisiana (September-October 1864)

Baker's Brigade, Liddell's Division, District of the Gulf, Department of Alabama, Mississippi and East Louisiana (October-December 1864)

Clanton's Brigade, District of the Gulf, Department of Alabama, Mississippi and East Louisiana (March 1865)

Battle: Mobile (March 17-April 12, 1865)

106.   ALABAMA 3RD INFANTRY REGIMENT

Organization: Organized at Montgomery on April 28, 1861. Mustered into Confederate service at Lynchburg, Virginia, on May 4, 1861. 1st Company G became the Montgomery True Blues Artillery Battery at Norfolk, Virginia, in January 1862. Surrendered at Appomattox Court House, Virginia, on April 9, 1865.

First Commander: Jones M. Withers (Colonel)

Field Officers: Cullen A. Battle (Major, Lieutenant Colonel, Colonel)

Charles Forsyth (Major, Lieutenant Colonel, Colonel)

Tennent Lomax (Lieutenant Colonel, Colonel)

Richard H. Powell (Major)

Robert M. Sands (Major, Lieutenant Colonel)

Assignments: Withers'-Mahone's Brigade, Department of Norfolk (December 1861-April 1862)

Mahone's Brigade, Huger's Division, Army of Northern Virginia (April-June 1862)

Rodes' Brigade, D. H. Hill's Division, Army of Northern Virginia (June-September 1862)

Rodes'-O'Neal's-Battle's Brigade, D. H. Hill's-Rodes' Division, 2nd Corps, Army of Northern Virginia (September 1862-June 1864)

Battle's Brigade, Rodes'-Ramseur's-Grimes' Division, Valley District, Department of Northern Virginia (June-December 1864)

Battle's Brigade, Grimes' Division, 2nd Corps, Army of Northern Virginia (December 1864-April 1865)

Battles: Seven Pines (May 31-June 1, 1862)

Seven Days Battles (June 25-July 1, 1862)

Gaines' Mill (June 27, 1862)

Malvern Hill (July 1, 1862)

South Mountain (September 14, 1862)

Antietam (September 17, 1862)

Fredericksburg (December 13, 1862)

Chancellorsville (May 1-4, 1863)
Gettysburg (July 1-3, 1863)
The Wilderness (May 5-6, 1864)
Spotsylvania Court House (May 8-21, 1864)
North Anna (May 23-26, 1864)
Cold Harbor (June 1-3, 1864)
Lynchburg Campaign (June 1864)
Monocacy (July 9, 1864)
3rd Winchester (September 19, 1864)
Fisher's Hill (September 22, 1864)
Cedar Creek (October 19, 1864)
Petersburg Siege (from December 1864) (June 1864-April 1865)
Fort Stedman (March 25, 1865)
Appomattox Court House (April 9, 1865)
Further Reading: Hotze, Henry. *Three Months in the Confederate Army.*

107. ALABAMA 3RD INFANTRY REGIMENT MILITIA

Organization: Mustered in with six companies on March 4, 1862. Mustered out by order of Brigadier General John H. Forney, commanding Department of Alabama and West Florida, on May 4, 1862.
First Commander: John Forsyth (Colonel)
Field Officers: Thomas K. Irwin (Major)
William A. LeBaron (Lieutenant Colonel)

108. ALABAMA 3RD INFANTRY REGIMENT RESERVES

Organization: Organized by the consolidation of independent companies, which had been mustered in between April 15 and July 27, 1864, on August 16, 1864. Surrendered by Lieutenant Richard Taylor, commanding the Department of Alabama, Mississippi and East Louisiana, at Citronelle, Alabama, on May 4, 1865.
First Commander: William M. Brooks (Colonel)
Field Officers: William D. Bulger (Major, Lieutenant Colonel)
Whitfield Walker (Major)
Assignments: Thomas' Brigade, District of the Gulf, Department of Alabama, Mississippi and East Louisiana (August-October 1864)
Post of Cahaba, Department of Alabama, Mississippi and East Louisiana (October-November 1864)
District of Central Alabama, Department of Alabama, Mississippi and East Louisiana (November 1864)
Clanton's Brigade, District of Central Alabama, Department of Alabama, Mississippi and East Louisiana (November-December 1864)

———— District of the Gulf, Department of Alabama, Mississippi and East
Louisiana (January-February 1865)
District of Central Alabama, Department of Alabama, Mississippi and East
Louisiana (February-March 1865)
District of Alabama, Department of Alabama, Mississippi and East Louisiana
(March-May 1865)

109. ALABAMA 4TH (CLIFTON'S) INFANTRY BATTALION

Also Known As: Alabama 10th Infantry Battalion
Organization: Organized with three companies on February 12, 1862. Redes-
ignated as the 16th Infantry Battalion on May 8, 1862.
First Commander: James M. Clifton (Major)
Assignments: Breckinridge's Brigade, Reserve, Central Army of Kentucky,
Department #2 (February-March 1862)
Trabue's Brigade, Reserve Corps, Army of the Mississippi, Department #2
(March-May 1862)
Battles: Shiloh (April 6-7, 1862)
Corinth Campaign (April-June 1862)

110. ALABAMA 4TH (CONOLEY'S) INFANTRY BATTALION

Organization: Organized with eight companies at Montgomery on November
16, 1861. Companies I and K assigned in February 1862. Designation changed
to 29th Infantry Regiment on March 10, 1862.
First Commander: Jonathan F. Conoley (Lieutenant Colonel)
Field Officer: Benjamin Morris (Major)
Assignment: Army of Pensacola, Department of Alabama and West Florida
(December 1861-March 1862)

111. ALABAMA 4TH INFANTRY BATTALION RESERVES

Organization: Organized in late 1864. Consolidated with the 3rd Infantry
Battalion Reserves and designated as the 65th Infantry Regiment in March
1865.
First Commander: (unidentified)
Assignments: Baker's Brigade, Liddell's Division, District of the Gulf, Depart-
ment of Alabama, Mississippi and East Louisiana (October-December 1864)
Clanton's Brigade, District of the Gulf, Department of Alabama, Mississippi
and East Louisiana (March 1865)
Battle: Mobile (March 17-April 12, 1865)

112. ALABAMA 4TH INFANTRY REGIMENT

Organization: Organized at Dallas, Georgia, on May 2, 1861. Mustered into Confederate service at Lynchburg, Virginia, on May 7, 1861. Surrendered at Appomattox Court House, Virginia, on April 9, 1865.

First Commander: Egbert J. Jones (Colonel)

Field Officers: Benjamin Allston (Major) (temporary appointment)
Pickney D. Bowles (Major, Lieutenant Colonel, Colonel)
Thomas K. Coleman (Major)
Thomas J. Goldsby (Lieutenant Colonel)
Evander McIvor Law (Lieutenant Colonel, Colonel)
Owen K. McLemore (Major, Lieutenant Colonel)
William M. Robbins (Major) (acting)
Charles L. Scott (Major)
Lawrence H. Scruggs (Major, Lieutenant Colonel)

Assignments: Army of the Shenandoah (May-June 1861)
Bee's Brigade, Army of the Shenandoah (June-July 1861)
Bee's-Whiting's Brigade, 2nd Corps, Army of the Potomac (July-October 1861)
Whiting's Brigade, G.W. Smith's-Whiting's Division, Department of Northern
    Virginia (October 1861-June 1862)
Whiting's Brigade, Whiting's Division, 2nd Corps, Army of Northern Virginia
    (June-July 1862)
Whiting's-Law's Brigade, Whiting's-Hood's Division, 1st Corps, Army of
    Northern Virginia (July 1862-February 1863)
Law's Brigade, Hood's Division, Department of North Carolina and Southern
    Virginia (February-April 1863)
Law's Brigade, Hood's Division, Department of Southern Virginia (April-May
    1863)
Law's Brigade, Hood's Division, 1st Corps, Army of Northern Virginia (May-
    September 1863)
Law's Brigade, Hood's Division, Longstreet's Corps, Army of Northern Virginia
    (September-November 1863)
Law's Brigade, Hood's-Field's Division, Department of East Tennessee (No-
    vember 1863-April 1864)
Law's-Perry's Brigade, Field's Division, 1st Corps, Army of Northern Virginia
    (April 1864-April 1865)

Battles: 1st Bull Run (July 21, 1861)
Seven Pines (May 31-June 1, 1862)
Seven Days Battles (June 25-July 1, 1862)
Gaines' Mill (June 27, 1862)
Malvern Hill (July 1, 1862)
2nd Bull Run (August 28-30, 1862)

South Mountain (September 14, 1862)
Antietam (September 17, 1862)
Fredericksburg (December 13, 1862)
Washington, North Carolina (March 30-April 14, 1863)
Suffolk Campaign (April-May 1863)
Gettysburg (July 1-3, 1863)
Chickamauga (September 19-20, 1863)
Chattanooga Siege (September-November 1863)
Wauhatchie (October 28-29, 1863)
Knoxville Siege (November 1863)
The Wilderness (May 5-6, 1864)
Spotsylvania Court House (May 8-21, 1864)
North Anna (May 23-26, 1864)
Cold Harbor (June 1-3, 1864)
Petersburg Siege (June 1864-April 1865)
Fort Harrison (September 29-30, 1864)
Fort Gilmer (September 29-30, 1864)
Appomattox Court House (April 9, 1865)
Further Reading: Pierrepont, Alice V. D. *Reuben Baughan Kidd, Soldier of the Confederacy.*

113. ALABAMA 4TH INFANTRY REGIMENT MILITIA

Organization: Organized on April 26, 1862 from 90-days companies organized at Mobile in March 1862. Mustered out in the summer of 1862.
First Commander: William M. Byrd (Colonel)

114. ALABAMA 4TH INFANTRY REGIMENT RESERVES

Organization: Organized by the increase of the 1st Infantry Battalion Reserves to a regiment in October 1864. Surrendered by Lieutenant Richard Taylor, commanding the Department of Alabama, Mississippi and East Louisiana, at Citronelle, Alabama, on May 4, 1865.
First Commander: William M. Stone (Colonel)
Field Officer: S. B. Waring (Major)
Assignments: Taylor's Brigade (Post of Mobile), District of the Gulf, Department of Alabama, Mississippi and East Louisiana (October-December 1864)
——— District of the Gulf, Department of Alabama, Mississippi and East Louisiana (January-February 1865)
District of Central Alabama, Department of Alabama, Mississippi and East Louisiana (February-March 1865)
District of Alabama, Department of Alabama, Mississippi and East Louisiana (March-May 1865)

115. ALABAMA 5TH INFANTRY BATTALION

Organization: Organized as the 8th Infantry Battalion with three companies for the war near Dumfries, Virginia, on December 2, 1861. Company K, 1st Tennessee Infantry Regiment, Provisional Army, assigned as Company D on February 8, 1862. Company E, a Florida unit, assigned in April 1862. Company F, an artillery unit, assigned in April or May 1862. Companies E and F became Companies L and M, 55th Virginia Infantry Regiment, respectively, on June 10, 1862. Battalion redesignated as the 5th Infantry Battalion on October 22, 1862. Company D disbanded on May 22, 1863. Surrendered at Appomattox Court House, Virginia, on April 9, 1865.

First Commander: F. B. Shepherd (Lieutenant Colonel) (temporary assignment)

Field Officers: Albert S. Van de Graaff (Major)
Henry H. Walker (Lieutenant Colonel) (temporary assignment)

Assignments: Wigfall's Brigade, Whiting's Division, Potomac District, Department of Northern Virginia (December 1861-April 1862)
Archer's Brigade, A. P. Hill's Division, Army of Northern Virginia (June-July 1862)
Archer's Brigade, A. P. Hill's Division, 1st Corps, Army of Northern Virginia (July 1862)
Archer's Brigade, A. P. Hill's Division, 2nd Corps, Army of Northern Virginia (July 1862-May 1863)
Archer's Brigade, Heth's Division, 3rd Corps, Army of Northern Virginia (May-July 1863)
Provost Guard, 3rd Corps, Army of Northern Virginia (July 1863-April 1865)

Battles: Union occupation of Fredericksburg, Virginia (April 19, 1862)
Seven Days Battles (June 25-July 1, 1862)
Mechanicsville (June 26, 1862)
Beaver Dam Creek (June 26, 1862)
Gaines' Mill (June 27, 1862)
Frayser's Farm (June 30, 1862)
Cedar Mountain (August 9, 1862)
2nd Bull Run (August 28-30, 1862)
Harpers Ferry (September 12-15, 1862)
Antietam (September 17, 1862)
Shepherdstown Ford (September 20, 1862)
Fredericksburg (December 13, 1862)
Chancellorsville (May 1-4, 1863)
Gettysburg (July 1-3, 1863)
Falling Waters (July 14, 1863)
Bristoe Campaign (October 1863)

Mine Run Campaign (November-December 1863)
The Wilderness (May 5-6, 1864)
Spotsylvania Court House (May 8-21, 1864)
North Anna (May 23-26, 1864)
Cold Harbor (June 1-3, 1864)
Petersburg Siege (June 1864-April 1865)
Appomattox Court House (April 9, 1865)
Further Reading: Fulton, William Frierson. *Family Record and War Reminiscences.*

116. ALABAMA 5TH (BLOUNT'S) INFANTRY BATTALION
See: ALABAMA 9TH (1ST ORGANIZATION) INFANTRY BATTALION

117. ALABAMA 5TH (GOLLADAY'S) INFANTRY BATTALION
Organization: Organized by the assignment of the three Alabama companies
of the 38th Tennessee Infantry Regiment at Corinth, Mississippi, in early
March 1862. Consolidated with the 2nd (Davis'-Chadwick's) Infantry Battal-
ion and designated as the 26th (Coltart's) Infantry Regiment (subsequently
50th Infantry Regiment) on April 3, 1862, per S.O. #27, 2nd Corps, Army of
the Mississippi, Department #2.
First Commander: Edward J. Golladay (Lieutenant Colonel)
Assignments: Walker's Brigade, 1st Corps, 2nd Grand Division, Army of the
Mississippi, Department #2 (March 1862)
Walker's Brigade, Ruggles' Division, 2nd Corps, Army of the Mississippi,
Department #2 (March-April 1862)

118. ALABAMA 5TH INFANTRY REGIMENT
Organization: Organized at Montgomery on May 5, 1862. 1st Company K
became Company A, Alabama State Artillery, on June 1, 1861. 1st Company
H became Fowler's Artillery Battery on December 28, 1861. Reorganized on
April 27, 1862. Surrendered at Appomattox Court House, Virginia, on April
9, 1865.
First Commander: Robert E. Rodes (Colonel)
Field Officers: Eugene Blackford (Major)
Josephus M. Hall (Lieutenant Colonel, Colonel)
Edwin L. Hobson (Lieutenant Colonel, Colonel)
Allen C. Jones (Lieutenant Colonel, Colonel)
John T. Morgan (Major, Lieutenant Colonel)
Christopher C. Pegues (Colonel)
Assignments: Department of Alexandria (June 1861)
Ewell's Brigade, Army of the Potomac (June-July 1861)

Ewell's Brigade, 1st Corps, Army of the Potomac (July-October 1861)
Ewell's Brigade, Van Dorn's Division, 1st Corps, Army of the Potomac (October 1861)
Ewell's-Rodes' Brigade, Van Dorn's-D. H. Hill's Division, Potomac District, Department of Northern Virginia (October 1861-March 1862)
Rodes' Brigade, D. H. Hill's Division, Army of Northern Virginia (March-September 1862)
Rodes'-Battle's Brigade, D. H. Hill's-Rodes' Division, 2nd Corps, Army of Northern Virginia (September 1862-June 1864)
Battle's Brigade, Rodes'-Grimes' Division, Valley District, Department of Northern Virginia (June-December 1864)
Battle's Brigade, Grimes' Division, 2nd Corps, Army of Northern Virginia (December 1864-April 1865)

Battles: Fairfax Court House (July 17, 1861)
1st Bull Run (July 21, 1861)
Williamsburg (May 5, 1862)
Seven Pines (May 31-June 1, 1862)
Seven Days Battles (June 25-July 1, 1862)
Gaines' Mill (June 27, 1862)
Malvern Hill (July 1, 1862)
South Mountain (September 14, 1862)
Antietam (September 17, 1862)
Fredericksburg (December 13, 1862)
Chancellorsville (May 1-4, 1863)
Gettysburg (July 1-3, 1863)
Manassas Gap (July 23, 1863)
Bristoe Campaign (October 1863)
Mine Run Campaign (November-December 1863)
The Wilderness (May 5-6, 1864)
Spotsylvania Court House (May 8-21, 1864)
North Anna (May 23-26, 1864)
Cold Harbor (June 1-3, 1864)
Lynchburg Campaign (June 1864)
Monocacy (July 9, 1864)
3rd Winchester (September 19, 1864)
Fisher's Hill (September 22, 1864)
Cedar Creek (October 19, 1864)
Petersburg Siege (from December 1864) (June 1864-April 1865)
Fort Stedman (March 25, 1865)
Appomattox Court House (April 9, 1865)

119. ALABAMA 6TH (MCCLELLAN'S) INFANTRY BATTALION

Organization: Organized with four companies in late 1861. Consolidated with the 1st (Loomis') Infantry Battalion and designated as the 25th Infantry Regiment on January 8, 1862.

First Commander: William B. McClellan (Lieutenant Colonel)

Assignment: District of Alabama, Department of Alabama and West Florida (December 1861-January 1862)

120. ALABAMA 6TH (NORWOOD'S) INFANTRY BATTALION

Organization: Organized by the assignment of the five Alabama companies of the 42nd Tennessee Infantry Regiment on October 9, 1862. Field consolidation with the 27th and 31st (Hale's) Infantry Regiments from October 1862 to January 1863. Consolidated with the 16th (Snodgrass') Infantry Battalion and designated as the 55th Infantry Regiment on February 23, 1863.

First Commander: Jonathan H. Norwood (Major, Lieutenant Colonel)

Assignments: (———— Brigade), Maury's Division, Army of West Tennessee, Department of Mississippi and East Louisiana (October-December 1862)

(———— Brigade), Maury's Division, 2nd Corps, Army of North Mississippi, Department of Mississippi and East Louisiana (December 1862-January 1863)

Beall's Brigade, 3rd Military District, Department of Mississippi and East Louisiana (January-February 1863)

121. ALABAMA 6TH INFANTRY REGIMENT

Organization: Organized at Montgomery on May 6, 1861. Reorganized on April 28, 1862. Surrendered at Appomattox Court House, Virginia, on April 9, 1865.

First Commander: John J. Seibels (Colonel)

Field Officers: Benjamin F. Baker (Lieutenant Colonel)

Isaac F. Culver (Major)

Augustus M. Gordon (Major, Lieutenant Colonel)

John B. Gordon (Major, Colonel)

George W. Hooper (Major, Lieutenant Colonel)

James N. Lightfoot (Lieutenant Colonel, Colonel)

Samuel P. Nesmith (Major)

Walter H. Weems (Major)

James J. Willingham (Lieutenant Colonel)

Assignments: Department of Alexandria (May-June 1861)
Ewell's Brigade, Army of the Potomac (June-July 1861)
Ewell's Brigade, 1st Corps, Army of the Potomac (July-October 1861)
Ewell's Brigade, Van Dorn's Division, 1st Corps, Army of the Potomac (October 1861)
Ewell's-Rodes' Brigade, Van Dorn's-D. H. Hill's Division, Potomac District, Department of Northern Virginia (October 1861-March 1862)
Rodes' Brigade, D. H. Hill's Division, Army of Northern Virginia (March-September 1862)
Rodes'-Battle's Brigade, D. H. Hill's-Rodes' Division, 2nd Corps, Army of Northern Virginia (September 1862-June 1864)
Battle's Brigade, Rodes'-Grimes' Division, Valley District, Department of Northern Virginia (June-December 1864)
Battle's Brigade, Grimes' Division, 2nd Corps, Army of Northern Virginia (December 1864-April 1865)

Battles: 1st Bull Run (July 21, 1861)
Williamsburg (May 5, 1862)
Seven Pines (May 31-June 1, 1862)
Seven Days Battles (June 25-July 1, 1862)
Gaines' Mill (June 27, 1862)
Malvern Hill (July 1, 1862)
South Mountain (September 14, 1862)
Antietam (September 17, 1862)
Fredericksburg (December 13, 1862)
Chancellorsville (May 1-4, 1863)
Gettysburg (July 1-3, 1863)
Manassas Gap (July 23, 1863)
Bristoe Campaign (October 1863)
Mine Run Campaign (November-December 1863)
The Wilderness (May 5-6, 1864)
Spotsylvania Court House (May 8-21, 1864)
North Anna (May 23-26, 1864)
Cold Harbor (June 1-3, 1864)
Lynchburg Campaign (June 1864)
Monocacy (July 9, 1864)
3rd Winchester (September 19, 1864)
Fisher's Hill (September 22, 1864)
Cedar Creek (October 19, 1864)
Petersburg Siege (from December 1864) (June 1864-April 1865)
Fort Stedman (March 25, 1865)
Appomattox Court House (April 9, 1865)

122. ALABAMA 7TH INFANTRY REGIMENT

Organization: Organized for 12 months from the 3rd (Coltart's) Infantry Battalion at Pensacola, Florida, on May 18, 1861. Companies H and I, cavalry companies, became Companies D and H, 3rd Cavalry Regiment, respectively. Disbanded in early April 1862.

First Commander: Sterling A. M. Wood (Colonel)

Field Officers: John G. Coltart (Lieutenant Colonel, Colonel)
Alfred A. Russell (Major)

Assignments: Troops at Pensacola, Florida (Bragg's Command) (May-October 1861)

Department of Alabama and West Florida (October 1861)

Army of Pensacola, Department of Alabama and West Florida (October-December 1861)

Wood's Brigade, Hardee's Division, Central Army of Kentucky, Department #2 (December 1861-February 1862)

Wood's Brigade, Pillow's Division, Central Army of Kentucky, Department #2 (February-March 1862)

Wood's Brigade, 3rd Corps, Army of the Mississippi, Department #2 (March-April 1862)

Battle: Santa Rosa Island (October 9, 1861)

123. ALABAMA 8TH INFANTRY BATTALION

See: ALABAMA 5TH INFANTRY BATTALION

124. ALABAMA 8TH INFANTRY REGIMENT

Organization: Organized for the war at Richmond, Virginia, on June 10, 1861. Surrendered at Appomattox Court House, Virginia, on April 9, 1865.

First Commander: John A. Winston (Colonel)

Field Officers: John P. Emrich (Major, Lieutenant Colonel)
John W. Frazer (Lieutenant Colonel)
Hilary A. Herbert (Major, Lieutenant Colonel, Colonel)
Thomas E. Irby (Major, Lieutenant Colonel)
Duke Nall (Major)
Young L. Royston (Major, Lieutenant Colonel, Colonel)

Assignments: Department of the Peninsula (June-October 1861)

Winston's Brigade, Department of the Peninsula (October 1861-January 1862)

McLaws' Division, Department of the Peninsula (January-February 1862)

Pryor's Brigade, Longstreet's Division, Department of Northern Virginia (April-June 1862)

Wilcox' Brigade, Longstreet's Division, Army of Northern Virginia (June 1862)

Wilcox's Brigade, Longstreet's Division, 1st Corps, Army of Northern Virginia (June-August 1862)

Wilcox's Brigade, Wilcox's Division, 1st Corps, Army of Northern Virginia (August-September 1862)

Wilcox's Brigade, Anderson's Division, 1st Corps, Army of Northern Virginia (September 1862-May 1863)

Wilcox's-Perrin's-Sanders'-Forney's Brigade, Anderson's-Mahone's Division, 3rd Corps, Army of Northern Virginia (May 1863-April 1865)

Battles: Yorktown Siege (April-May 1862)

Williamsburg (May 5, 1862)

Seven Pines (May 31-June 1, 1862)

Seven Days Battles (June 25-July 1, 1862)

Gaines' Mill (June 27, 1862)

Frayser's Farm (June 30, 1862)

2nd Bull Run (August 28-30, 1862)

Harpers Ferry (September 12-15, 1862)

Antietam (September 17, 1862)

Fredericksburg (December 13, 1862)

Chancellorsville (May 1-4, 1863)

Gettysburg (July 1-3, 1863)

Bristoe Campaign (October 1863)

Mine Run Campaign (November-December 1863)

The Wilderness (May 5-6, 1864)

Spotsylvania Court House (May 8-21, 1864)

North Anna (May 23-26, 1864)

Cold Harbor (June 1-3, 1864)

Petersburg Siege (June 1864-April 1865)

The Crater (July 30, 1864)

Appomattox Court House (April 9, 1865)

125. ALABAMA 9TH (1ST ORGANIZATION) INFANTRY BATTALION

Also Known As: Alabama 5th (Blount's) Infantry Battalion

Organization: Organized with eight companies on March 1, 1862. Disbanded and the men transferred to the 17th and 18th Infantry Regiments on April 28, 1862.

First Commander: Robert P. Blount (Lieutenant Colonel)

Field Officer: William D. C. Lloyd (Major)

Assignment: Jackson's Brigade, Withers' Division, 2nd Corps, Army of the Mississippi, Department #2 (April 1862)

Battle: Shiloh (April 6-7, 1862)

126. ALABAMA 9TH (2ND ORGANIZATION) INFANTRY BATTALION

Organization: Organized with eight companies on March 2, 1863. Company I assigned on June 20, 1863. Increased to a regiment by the assignment of Company E, 2nd (Cox') Georgia Sharpshooters Battalion, as Company K on June 28, 1863. Designation changed to the 58th Infantry Regiment on August 13, 1863.

First Commander: Bushrod Jones (Lieutenant Colonel)

Field Officers: John W. Inger (Major)

J. M. Thomason (Major)

Assignments: Slaughter's Brigade, District of the Gulf, Department #2 (March-April 1863)

Slaughter's Brigade, Western Division, Department of the Gulf (April 1863)

Bate's Brigade, Stewart's Division, 2nd Corps, Army of Tennessee (June-August 1863)

Battles: Tullahoma Campaign (June 1863)

Hoover's Gap (June 24, 1863)

127. ALABAMA 9TH INFANTRY REGIMENT

Organization: Organized at Richmond, Virginia, on June 20, 1861. Surrendered at Appomattox Court House, Virginia, on April 9, 1865.

First Commander: Cadmus M. Wilcox (Colonel)

Field Officers: James M. Crow (Major)

Stephen F. Hale (Lieutenant Colonel) (temporary assignment)

Samuel Henry (Lieutenant Colonel, Colonel)

J. Horace King (Major, Colonel)

Edward A. O'Neal (Lieutenant Colonel)

Gaynes C. Smith (Lieutenant Colonel)

Jere H. J. Williams (Major)

Assignments: E. K. Smith's Brigade, Army of the Shenandoah (July 1861)

E. K. Smith's Brigade, 2nd Corps, Army of the Potomac (July-October 1861)

E. K. Smith's-Wilcox's Brigade, G.W. Smith's Division, Potomac District, Department of Northern Virginia (October 1861-January 1862)

Wilcox's Brigade, Longstreet's Division, Army of Northern Virginia (April-June 1862)

Wilcox's Brigade, Longstreet's Division, 1st Corps, Army of Northern Virginia (June-August 1862)

Wilcox's Brigade, Wilcox's Division, 1st Corps, Army of Northern Virginia (August-September 1862)

Wilcox's Brigade, Anderson's Division, 1st Corps, Army of Northern Virginia (September 1862-May 1863)

Wilcox's-Perrin's-Sanders'-Forney's Brigade, Anderson's-Mahone's Division, 3rd Corps, Army of Northern Virginia (May 1863-April 1865)
Battles: Yorktown Siege (April-May 1862)
Williamsburg (May 5, 1862)
Seven Pines (May 31-June 1, 1862)
Seven Days Battles (June 25-July 1, 1862)
Gaines' Mill (June 27, 1862)
Frayser's Farm (June 30, 1862)
2nd Bull Run (August 28-30, 1862)
Harpers Ferry (September 12-15, 1862)
Antietam (September 17, 1862)
Fredericksburg (December 13, 1862)
Chancellorsville (May 1-4, 1863)
Gettysburg (July 1-3, 1863)
Bristoe Campaign (October 1863)
Mine Run Campaign (November-December 1863)
The Wilderness (May 5-6, 1864)
Spotsylvania Court House (May 8-21, 1864)
North Anna (May 23-26, 1864)
Cold Harbor (June 1-3, 1864)
Petersburg Siege (June 1864-April 1865)
The Crater (July 30, 1864)
Appomattox Court House (April 9, 1865)

128. ALABAMA 10TH INFANTRY BATTALION
See: ALABAMA 4TH (CLIFTON'S) INFANTRY BATTALION

129. ALABAMA 10TH INFANTRY REGIMENT
Organization: Organized at Montgomery on June 4, 1861. Surrendered at Appomattox Court House, Virginia, on April 9, 1865.
First Commander: John H. Forney (Colonel)
Field Officers: Taul Bradford (Major)
John H. Caldwell (Major, Lieutenant Colonel)
Arthur S. Cunningham (Lieutenant Colonel) (temporary assignment)
William H. Forney (Major, Lieutenant Colonel, Colonel)
Lewis W. Johnson (Major)
James B. Martin (Lieutenant Colonel)
James E. Shelley (Lieutenant Colonel)
William T. Smith (Lieutenant Colonel)
James H. Truss (Major)
John J. Woodward (Major, Lieutenant Colonel, Colonel)

Assignments: E. K. Smith's Brigade, Army of the Shenandoah (July 1861)
E. K. Smith's Brigade, 2nd Corps, Army of the Potomac (July-October 1861)
E. K. Smith's-Wilcox's Brigade, G.W. Smith's Division, Potomac District,
   Department of Northern Virginia (October 1861-January 1862)
Wilcox's Brigade, Longstreet's Division, Army of Northern Virginia (April-
   June 1862)
Wilcox's Brigade, Longstreet's Division, 1st Corps, Army of Northern
   Virginia (June-August 1862)
Wilcox's Brigade, Wilcox's Division, 1st Corps, Army of Northern Virginia
   (August-September 1862)
Wilcox's Brigade, Anderson's Division, 1st Corps, Army of Northern Vir-
   ginia (September 1862-May 1863)
Wilcox's-Perrin's-Sanders'-Forney's Brigade, Anderson's-Mahone's Divi-
   sion, 3rd Corps, Army of Northern Virginia (May 1863-April 1865)
Battles: Dranesville (December 20, 1861)
Yorktown Siege (April-May 1862)
Williamsburg (May 5, 1862)
Seven Pines (May 31-June 1, 1862)
Seven Days Battles (June 25-July 1, 1862)
Gaines' Mill (June 27, 1862)
Frayser's Farm (June 30, 1862)
2nd Bull Run (August 28-30, 1862)
Harpers Ferry (September 12-15, 1862)
Antietam (September 17, 1862)
Fredericksburg (December 13, 1862)
Chancellorsville (May 1-4, 1863)
Gettysburg (July 1-3, 1863)
Bristoe Campaign (October 1863)
Mine Run Campaign (November-December 1863)
The Wilderness (May 5-6, 1864)
Spotsylvania Court House (May 8-21, 1864)
North Anna (May 23-26, 1864)
Cold Harbor (June 1-3, 1864)
Petersburg Siege (June 1864-April 1865)
Appomattox Court House (April 9, 1865)

130. ALABAMA 11TH INFANTRY REGIMENT

Organization: Organized at Lynchburg, Virginia, on June 11, 1861. Surren-
dered at Appomattox Court House, Virginia, on April 9, 1865.
First Commander: Sydenham Moore (Colonel)
Field Officers: George Field (Major)

Richard J. Fletcher (Major)
Archibald Gracie, Jr. (Major)
Stephen F. Hale (Lieutenant Colonel)
John C. C. Sanders (Colonel)
George E. Tayloe (Lieutenant Colonel, Colonel)
Assignments: E. K. Smith's Brigade, Army of the Shenandoah (July 1861)
E. K. Smith's Brigade, 2nd Corps, Army of the Potomac (July-October 1861)
E. K. Smith's-Wilcox's Brigade, G. W. Smith's Division, Potomac District,
 Department of Northern Virginia (October 1861-January 1862)
Wilcox's Brigade, Longstreet's Division, Army of Northern Virginia (April-
 June 1862)
Wilcox's Brigade, Longstreet's Division, 1st Corps, Army of Northern Virginia
 (June-August 1862)
Wilcox's Brigade, Wilcox's Division, 1st Corps, Army of Northern Virginia
 (August-September 1862)
Wilcox's Brigade, Anderson's Division, 1st Corps, Army of Northern Virginia
 (September 1862-May 1863)
Wilcox's-Perrin's-Sanders'-Forney's Brigade, Anderson's-Mahone's Division,
 3rd Corps, Army of Northern Virginia (May 1863-April 1865)
Battles: Yorktown Siege (April-May 1862)
Williamsburg (May 5, 1862)
Seven Pines (May 31-June 1, 1862)
Seven Days Battles (June 25-July 1, 1862)
Gaines' Mill (June 27, 1862)
Frayser's Farm (June 30, 1862)
2nd Bull Run (August 28-30, 1862)
Harpers Ferry (September 12-15, 1862)
Antietam (September 17, 1862)
Fredericksburg (December 13, 1862)
Chancellorsville (May 1-4, 1863)
Gettysburg (July 1-3, 1863)
Bristoe Campaign (October 1863)
Mine Run Campaign (November-December 1863)
The Wilderness (May 5-6, 1864)
Spotsylvania Court House (May 8-21, 1864)
North Anna (May 23-26, 1864)
Cold Harbor (June 1-3, 1864)
Petersburg Siege (June 1864-April 1865)
The Crater (July 30, 1864)
Appomattox Court House (April 9, 1865)

Further Reading: Clark, George. *A Glance Backward; or, Some Events in the Past History of My Life.*

131. ALABAMA 12TH INFANTRY REGIMENT

Organization: Organized at Richmond, Virginia, on July 17, 1861. Reorganized on April 28, 1862. Surrendered at Appomattox Court House, Virginia, on April 9, 1865.

First Commander: Robert T. Jones (Colonel)

Field Officers: John C. Brown (Major)
Bristor B. Gayle (Colonel)
John C. Goodgame (Major, Lieutenant Colonel)
Theodore O'Hara (Lieutenant Colonel)
Samuel B. Pickens (Lieutenant Colonel, Colonel)
Adolphus Proskauer (Major)
Augustus Stikes (Major)
Edward D. Tracy (Major)

Assignments: Ewell's Brigade, 1st Corps, Army of the Potomac (July-October 1861)
Rodes' Brigade, Van Dorn's-D. H. Hill's Division, Potomac District, Department of Northern Virginia (October 1861-March 1862)
Rodes' Brigade, D. H. Hill's Division, Army of Northern Virginia (March-September 1862)
Rodes'-O'Neal's-Battle's Brigade, D. H. Hill's-Rodes' Division, 2nd Corps, Army of Northern Virginia (September 1862-June 1864)
Battle's Brigade, Rodes'-Ramseur's-Grimes' Division, Valley District, Department of Northern Virginia (June-December 1864)
Battle's Brigade, Grimes' Division, 2nd Corps, Army of Northern Virginia (December 1864-April 1865)

Battles: Yorktown Siege (April-May 1862)
Williamsburg (May 5, 1862)
Seven Pines (May 31-June 1, 1862)
Seven Days Battles (June 25-July 1, 1862)
Gaines' Mill (June 27, 1862)
Malvern Hill (July 1, 1862)
South Mountain (September 14, 1862)
Antietam (September 17, 1862)
Fredericksburg (December 13, 1862)
Chancellorsville (May 1-4, 1863)
Gettysburg (July 1-3, 1863)
The Wilderness (May 5-6, 1864)
Spotsylvania Court House (May 8-21, 1864)

North Anna (May 23-26, 1864)
Cold Harbor (June 1-3, 1864)
Lynchburg Campaign (June 1864)
Monocacy (July 9, 1864)
3rd Winchester (September 19, 1864)
Fisher's Hill (September 22, 1864)
Cedar Creek (October 19, 1864)
Petersburg Siege (from December 1864) (June 1864-April 1865)
Fort Stedman (March 25, 1865)
Appomattox Court House (April 9, 1865)
Further Reading: Park, Robert Emory. *Sketch of the Twelfth Alabama Infantry of Battle's Brigade, Rode's Division, Early's Corps, of the Army of North Virginia.*

132. ALABAMA 13TH INFANTRY REGIMENT

Organization: Organized at Montgomery on July 19, 1861. Mustered in on July 19 and 26, 1861. Surrendered at Appomattox Court House, Virginia, on April 9, 1865.
First Commander: Birkett D. Fry (Colonel)
Field Officers: James Aiken (Major, Lieutenant Colonel, Colonel)
William H. Betts (Major, Lieutenant Colonel)
Reginald H. Dawson (Major, Lieutenant Colonel)
Samuel B. Marks (Major, Lieutenant Colonel)
Julius C. B. Mitchell (Lieutenant Colonel)
John T. Smith (Major)
Assignments: Department of the Peninsula (September-October 1861)
Winston's Brigade, Department of the Peninsula (October 1861)
Rains' Division, Department of the Peninsula (January-April 1862)
Rains'-Colquitt's Brigade, D. H. Hill's Division, Army of Northern Virginia (April-September 1862)
Colquitt's Brigade, D. H. Hill's Division, 2nd Corps, Army of Northern Virginia (September 1862-January 1863)
Archer's Brigade, A. P. Hill's Division, 2nd Corps, Army of Northern Virginia (January-May 1863)
Archer's-Fry's Brigade, Heth's Division, 3rd Corps, Army of Northern Virginia (May 1863-January 1865)
Sanders'-Forney's Brigade, Mahone's Division, 3rd Corps, Army of Northern Virginia (January-April 1865)
Battles: Yorktown Siege (April-May 1862)
Williamsburg (May 5, 1862)
Seven Pines (May 31-June 1, 1862)
Seven Days Battles (June 25-July 1, 1862)

Gaines' Mill (June 27, 1862)
Malvern Hill (July 1, 1862)
South Mountain (September 14, 1862)
Antietam (September 17, 1862)
Fredericksburg (December 13, 1862)
Chancellorsville (May 1-4, 1863)
Gettysburg (July 1-3, 1863)
Falling Waters (July 14, 1863)
Bristoe Campaign (October 1863)
Mine Run Campaign (November-December 1863)
The Wilderness (May 5-6, 1864)
Spotsylvania Court House (May 8-21, 1864)
North Anna (May 23-26, 1864)
Cold Harbor (June 1-3, 1864)
Petersburg Siege (June 1864-April 1865)
Squirrel Level Road (September 30, 1864)
Jones' Farm (September 30, 1864)
Pegram's Farm (October 1, 1864)
Harman Road (October 2, 1864)
Appomattox Court House (April 9, 1865)

133. ALABAMA 14TH INFANTRY REGIMENT

Organization: Organized in state service at Auburn on July 19, 1861. Mustered into Confederate service there on August 7, 1861. Surrendered at Appomattox Court House, Virginia, on April 9, 1865.
First Commander: Thomas R. Judge (Colonel)
Field Officers: David W. Baine (Lieutenant Colonel)
James A. Broome (Major, Lieutenant Colonel)
Mickleberry P. Ferrell (Major)
Robert A. McCord (Major)
Owen K. McLemore (Major)
Lucius Pinckard (Lieutenant Colonel, Colonel)
George W. Taylor (Major)
Alfred C. Wood (Major, Lieutenant Colonel, Colonel)
Assignments: Walker's Brigade, Department #1 (September-November 1861)
(——— Brigade, ——— Division), Potomac District, Department of Northern Virginia (November 1861-January 1862)
at Richmond recovering from camp disease (January-March 1862)
Pryor's Brigade, Longstreet's Division, Army of Northern Virginia (April-June 1862)

Pryor's Brigade, Longstreet's Division, 1st Corps, Army of Northern Virginia
(June-August 1862)
Pryor's Brigade, Wilcox's Division, 1st Corps, Army of Northern Virginia
(August-September 1862)
Pryor's Brigade, Anderson's Division, 1st Corps, Army of Northern Virginia
(September-November 1862)
Wilcox's Brigade, Anderson's Division, 1st Corps, Army of Northern Virginia
(November 1862-May 1863)
Wilcox's-Perrin's-Sanders'-Forney's Brigade, Anderson's-Mahone's Division,
3rd Corps, Army of Northern Virginia (May 1863-April 1865)
Battles: Yorktown Siege (April-May 1862)
Lee's Mill (April 5, 1862)
Williamsburg (May 5, 1862)
Seven Pines (May 31-June 1, 1862)
Seven Days Battles (June 25-July 1, 1862)
Gaines' Mill (June 27, 1862)
Frayser's Farm (June 30, 1862)
2nd Bull Run (August 28-30, 1862)
Harpers Ferry (September 12-15, 1862)
Antietam (September 17, 1862)
Fredericksburg (December 13, 1862)
Chancellorsville (May 1-4, 1863)
Gettysburg (July 1-3, 1863)
Bristoe Campaign (October 1863)
Mine Run Campaign (November-December 1863)
The Wilderness (May 5-6, 1864)
Spotsylvania Court House (May 8-21, 1864)
North Anna (May 23-26, 1864)
Cold Harbor (June 1-3, 1864)
Petersburg Siege (June 1864-April 1865)
Appomattox Court House (April 9, 1865)
Further Reading: Hurst, Marshall B. *History of the Fourteenth Alabama Volunteers: With a List of the Names of Every Man That Ever Belonged to the Regiment.*

134. ALABAMA 15TH INFANTRY REGIMENT

Organization: Organized in state service at Fort Mitchell on July 3, 1861.
Organized in Confederate service on July 27, 1861. Mustered into Confederate
service for the war on August 2, 1861. Surrendered at Appomattox Court
House, Virginia, on April 9, 1865.
First Commander: James Cantey (Colonel)
Field Officers: John W. L. Daniel (Major)

Isaac B. Feagin (Lieutenant Colonel)
Alexander A. Lowther (Major, Colonel)
William C. Oates (Major, Lieutenant Colonel, Colonel)
John F. Treutlen (Lieutenant Colonel, Colonel)
Assignments: (——— Brigade, ——— Corps), Army of the Potomac (August-October 1861)
Trimble's Brigade, E. K. Smith's-Ewell's Division, Potomac District, Department of Northern Virginia (October 1861-April 1862)
Trimble's Brigade, Ewell's Division, Department of Northern Virginia (April-May 1862)
Trimble's Brigade, Ewell's Division, Valley District, Department of Northern Virginia (May-June 1862)
Trimble's Brigade, Ewell's Division, 2nd Corps, Army of Northern Virginia (June 1862-January 1863)
Law's Brigade, Hood's Division, 1st Corps, Army of Northern Virginia (January-February 1863)
Law's Brigade, Hood's Division, Department of North Carolina and Southern Virginia (February-April 1863)
Law's Brigade, Hood's Division, Department of Southern Virginia (April-May 1863)
Law's Brigade, Hood's Division, 1st Corps, Army of Northern Virginia (May-September 1863)
Law's Brigade, Hood's Division, Longstreet's Corps, Army of Tennessee (September-November 1863)
Law's Brigade, Hood's-Field's Division, Department of East Tennessee (November 1863-April 1864)
Law's-Perry's Brigade, Field's Division, 1st Corps, Army of Northern Virginia (April 1864-April 1865)

Battles: Shenandoah Valley Campaign of 1862 (May-June 1862)
Front Royal (May 23, 1862)
1st Winchester (May 25, 1862)
Cross Keys (June 8, 1862)
Seven Days Battles (June 25-July 1, 1862)
Gaines' Mill (June 27, 1862)
Malvern Hill (July 1, 1862)
Cedar Mountain (August 9, 1862)
Rappahannock Station (August 23, 1862)
Hazel River (August 22, 1862)
2nd Bull Run (August 28-30, 1862)
Chantilly (September 1, 1862)
Antietam (September 17, 1862)

Boteler's Ford (September 19, 1862)
Shepherdstown Ford (September 20, 1862)
Fredericksburg (December 13, 1862)
Suffolk Campaign (April-May 1863)
Gettysburg (July 1-3, 1863)
Chickamauga (September 19-20, 1863)
Chattanooga Siege (September-November 1863)
Wauhatchie (October 28-29, 1863)
Knoxville Siege (November 1863)
Bean's Station (December 15, 1863)
The Wilderness (May 5-6, 1864)
Spotsylvania Court House (May 8-21, 1864)
North Anna (May 23-26, 1864)
Cold Harbor (June 1-3, 1864)
Petersburg Siege (June 1864-April 1865)
Fort Harrison (September 29-30, 1864)
Fort Gilmer (September 29-30, 1864)
Darbytown Road (October 7, 1864)
Darbytown Road (October 13, 1864)
Appomattox Court House (April 9, 1865)
Further Reading: Oates, William C. *The War Between the Union and the Confederacy and Its Lost Opportunities with a History of the Fifteenth Alabama Regiment and the Forty-eight Battles in Which It Fought.*

135. ALABAMA 16TH (SNODGRASS') INFANTRY BATTALION

Organization: Organized by the addition of four companies to the 4th (Clifton's) Infantry Battalion on May 8, 1862. Consolidated with the 6th (Norwood's) Infantry Battalion and designated as the 55th Infantry Regiment at Port Hudson, Louisiana, on February 23, 1863.

First Commander: John Snodgrass (Lieutenant Colonel)

Field Officers: G. L. Alexander (Major)
John H. Gibson (Major)

Assignments: Hawes' Brigade, Reserve Corps, Army of the Mississippi, Department #2 (May-June 1862)
Hawes' Brigade, Breckinridge's Command, District of the Mississippi, Department #2 (June-July 1862)
Helm's Brigade, Clark's Division, Breckinridge's Command, District of the Mississippi, Department #2 (July-August 1862)
Rust's Brigade, Lovell's Division, District of the Mississippi, Department #2 (August-October 1862)

————— Maury's Division, Army of West Tennessee, Department of Mississippi
and East Louisiana (October-December 1862)
————— Rust's Division, 1st Corps, Army of North Mississippi, Department of
Mississippi and East Louisiana (December 1862-January 1863)
Beall's Brigade, 3rd Military District, Department of Mississippi and East
Louisiana (January-February 1863)
Battles: Corinth Campaign (April-June 1862)
Vicksburg Bombardments (May 18-July 27, 1862)
Baton Rouge (August 5, 1862)
Corinth (October 3-4, 1862)

136.   ALABAMA 16TH INFANTRY REGIMENT

Organization: Organized at Courtland in August 1861. Field consolidation
with the 33rd and 45th Infantry Regiments from late 1864 to April 8, 1865.
Consolidated with the 1st, 33rd and 45th Infantry Regiments and designated
as the 1st Infantry Regiment Consolidated at Smithfield, North Carolina, on
April 8, 1865.
First Commander: William B. Wood (Colonel)
Field Officers: Frederic A. Ashford (Lieutenant Colonel, Colonel)
John W. Harris (Lieutenant Colonel)
Alexander H. Helvenston (Major, Lieutenant Colonel, Colonel)
John H. McGaughy (Major, Lieutenant Colonel)
Joseph J. May (Major, Lieutenant Colonel)
Assignments: District of East Tennessee, Department #2 (September 1861-
January 1862)
Carroll's Brigade, District of East Tennessee, Department #2 (January 1862)
Wood's Brigade, Pillow's Division, Central Army of Kentucky, Department #2
(February-March 1862)
Wood's Brigade, 3rd Corps, Army of the Mississippi, Department #2 (March-
July 1862)
Wood's Brigade, Hardee's Division, Army of the Mississippi, Department #2
(July-August 1862)
Wood's Brigade, Buckner's Division, Left Wing, Army of the Mississippi,
Department #2 (August-November 1862)
Wood's-Lowrey's Brigade, Buckner's-Cleburne's Division, 2nd Corps, Army of
Tennessee (November 1862-November 1863)
Lowrey's Brigade, Cleburne's Division, 1st Corps, Army of Tennessee (Novem-
ber 1863-April 1865)
Battles: Mill Springs (January 19, 1862)
Shiloh (April 6-7, 1862)
Perryville (October 8, 1862)

Triune (December 1862)
Murfreesboro (December 31, 1862-January 3, 1863)
Tullahoma Campaign (June 1863)
Ringgold Gap (November 27, 1863)
Buzzard Roost Gap (February 25, 1864)
Atlanta Campaign (May-September 1864)
Dalton (May 5-11, 1864)
Resaca (May 14-15, 1864)
Adairsville (May 15-18, 1864)
Cassville (May 19-22, 1864)
New Hope Church (May 25-June 4, 1864)
Pickett's Mills (May 27, 1864)
Kennesaw Mountain (June 27, 1864)
Peach Tree Creek (July 20, 1864)
Atlanta (July 22, 1864)
Atlanta Siege (July-September 1864)
Jonesboro (August 31-September 1, 1864)
Franklin (November 30, 1864)
Nashville (December 15-16, 1864)
Carolinas Campaign (February-April 1865)

137. ALABAMA 17TH INFANTRY BATTALION SHARPSHOOTERS

Organization: Organized with two companies by the assignment of detachments from the 19th and 39th Infantry Regiments in June 1862. Disappears from the records in August 1864 with the men possibly returned to their original commands.

First Commander: Benjamin C. Yancey (Lieutenant Colonel)

Assignments: Gardner's Brigade, Reserve Corps, Army of the Mississippi, Department #2 (June-July 1862)

Gardner's Brigade, Reserve Division, Army of the Mississippi, Department #2 (July-August 1862)

Gardner's Brigade, Withers' Division, Right Wing, Army of the Mississippi, Department #2 (August-November 1862)

Gardner's-Deas' Brigade, Withers'-Hindman's Division, 1st Corps, Army of Tennessee (November 1862-November 1863)

Deas'-Johnston's Brigade, Hindman's-Anderson's-Johnson's Division, 2nd Corps, Army of Tennessee (November 1863-August 1864)

Battles: Murfreesboro (December 31, 1862-January 3, 1863)

Chickamauga (September 19-20, 1863)

Chattanooga Siege (September-November 1863)

Chattanooga (November 23-25, 1863)

Atlanta Campaign (May-September 1864)
New Hope Church (May 25-June 4, 1864)
Atlanta Siege (July-September 1864)

138. ALABAMA 17TH INFANTRY REGIMENT

Organization: Organized at Montgomery on September 5, 1861. Mustered into Confederate service in September 1861. Field consolidation with the 1st and 29th Infantry Regiments in early 1865. Consolidated with the 33rd Infantry Regiment and designated as the 17th Infantry Regiment Consolidated on April 20, 1865.

First Commander: Thomas H. Watts (Colonel)

Field Officers: Thomas J. Burnett (Major)
Robert C. Fariss (Lieutenant Colonel, Colonel)
Edward P. Holcombe (Lieutenant Colonel)
Joseph P. Jones (Colonel)
Stephen A. Moreno (Major) (temporary assignment)
Virgil S. Murphey (Major, Colonel)
John Ryan (Lieutenant Colonel) (temporary assignment)

Assignments: Walker's Brigade, Department #1 (September-October 1861)
Department of West Florida (October 1861)
Department of Alabama and West Florida (October 1861)
Army of Pensacola, Department of Alabama and West Florida (October 1861-March 1862)
Jackson's Brigade, Withers' Division, 2nd Corps, Army of the Mississippi, Department #2 (March-June 1862)
Jackson's Brigade, Reserve Corps, Army of the Mississippi, Department #2 (June-July 1862)
Jackson's Brigade, Reserve Division, Army of the Mississippi, Department #2 (July 1862)
Army of Mobile, District of the Gulf, Department #2 (October 1862-April 1863)
Slaughter's Brigade, Western Division, Department of the Gulf (April-May 1863)
Slaughter's Brigade, Department of the Gulf (June 1863)
Cantey's Brigade, Western Division, Department of the Gulf (July-September 1863)
Cantey's Brigade, Department of the Gulf (September 1863-March 1864)
Cantey's Brigade, Army of Tennessee (April-May 1864)
Cantey's Brigade, Cantey's-Walthall's Division, Army of Mississippi (May-July 1864)
Cantey's-Shelley's Brigade, Walthall's Division, 3rd Corps, Army of Tennessee (July-December 1864)

Quarles' Brigade, Walthall's Division, 3rd Corps, Army of Tennessee (March-April 1865)
Shelley's Brigade, Loring's Division, 3rd Corps, Army of Tennessee (April 1865)
Battles: Pensacola (October 9, 1861)
Shiloh (April 6-7, 1862)
Atlanta Campaign (May-September 1864)
Resaca (May 14-15, 1864)
Cassville (May 19-22, 1864)
Kennesaw Mountain (June 27, 1864)
Peach Tree Creek (July 20, 1864)
Atlanta (July 22, 1864)
Ezra Church (July 28, 1864)
Atlanta Siege (July-September 1864)
Jonesboro (August 31-September 1, 1864)
Lovejoy's Station (September 2-5, 1864)
Franklin (November 30, 1864)
Nashville (December 15-16, 1864)
Carolinas Campaign (February-April 1865)

139. ALABAMA 17TH INFANTRY REGIMENT CONSOLIDATED
Organization: Organized by the consolidation of the 17th and 33rd Infantry Regiments on April 20, 1865. Surrendered by General Joseph E. Johnston at Durham Station, Orange County, North Carolina, on April 26, 1865.
First Commander: Edward P. Holcombe (Colonel)
Assignment: Shelley's Brigade, Loring's Division, 3rd Corps, Army of Tennessee (April 1865)
Battle: Carolinas Campaign (February-April 1865)

140. ALABAMA 18TH INFANTRY BATTALION
Also Known As: 18th Partisan Rangers Battalion
Organization: Organized with three companies by the change of designation of the 1st Partisan Rangers Battalion some time in late 1862 or early 1863. Field consolidation with the 33rd Infantry Regiment in early 1863. Merged into the 33rd Infantry Regiment in late 1863.
First Commander: William T. Gunter (Major)
Field Officer: J. H. Gibson (Major)
Assignment: Wood's-Lowrey's Brigade, Cleburne's Division, 2nd Corps, Army of Tennessee (September-November 1863)
Battles: Chickamauga (September 19-20, 1863)
Chattanooga Siege (September-November 1863)

Chattanooga (November 23-25, 1863)

141. ALABAMA 18TH INFANTRY REGIMENT

Organization: Organized at Huntsville on September 4, 1861. Surrendered by Lieutenant Richard Taylor, commanding the Department of Alabama, Mississippi and East Louisiana, at Meridian, Mississippi, on May 4, 1865.
First Commander: Edward C. Bullock (Colonel)
Field Officers: James T. Holtzclaw (Major, Lieutenant Colonel, Colonel)
Peter F. Hunley (Major, Lieutenant Colonel)
Richard F. Inge (Lieutenant Colonel)
William M. Moxley (Major)
Shep. Ruffin (Major)
Eli S. Shorter (Lieutenant Colonel, Colonel)
James Strawbridge (Colonel) (temporary assignment)
Bryan M. Thomas (Major) (temporary assignment)
Assignments: Walker's Brigade, Department #1 (September-October 1861)
District of Alabama, Department of Alabama and West Florida (October 1861-January 1862)
Army of Mobile, Department of Alabama and West Florida (January-February 1862)
2nd Brigade, 2nd Division, 2nd Grand Division, Army of the Mississippi, Department #2 (March 1862)
Jackson's Brigade, Withers' Division, 2nd Corps, Army of the Mississippi, Department #2 (March-June 1862)
Jackson's Brigade, Reserve Corps, Army of the Mississippi, Department #2 (June-July 1862)
Jackson's Brigade, Reserve Division, Army of the Mississippi, Department #2 (July 1862)
Army of Mobile, District of the Gulf, Department #2 (July 1862-April 1863)
Cumming's Brigade, Western Division, Department of the Gulf (April 1863)
Clayton's Brigade, Stewart's Division, 2nd Corps, Army of Tennessee (April-September 1863)
Clayton's Brigade, Stewart's Division, Buckner's Corps, Army of Tennessee (September-October 1863)
Clayton's-Holtzclaw's Brigade, Stewart's-Clayton's Division, 2nd Corps, Army of Tennessee (October 1863-January 1865)
Holtzclaw's Brigade, District of the Gulf, Department of Alabama, Mississippi and East Louisiana (January-April 1865)
Holtzclaw's Brigade, Department of Alabama, Mississippi and East Louisiana (April-May 1865)
Battles: Shiloh (April 6-7, 1862)

Corinth Campaign (April-June 1862)
Tullahoma Campaign (June 1863)
Chickamauga (September 19-20, 1863)
Chattanooga Siege (September-November 1863)
Chattanooga (November 23-25, 1863)
Atlanta Campaign (May-September 1864)
Dalton (May 5-11, 1864)
Resaca (May 14-15, 1864)
Cassville (May 19-22, 1864)
New Hope Church (May 25-June 4, 1864)
Pickett's Mills (May 27, 1864)
Peach Tree Creek (July 20, 1864)
Atlanta (July 22, 1864)
Ezra Church (July 28, 1864)
Atlanta Siege (July-September 1864)
Jonesboro (August 31-September 1, 1864)
Lovejoy's Station (September 2-5, 1864)
Franklin (not engaged) (November 30, 1864)
Nashville (December 15-16, 1864)
Mobile (March 17-April 12, 1865)

142. ALABAMA 19TH INFANTRY REGIMENT

Organization: Organized at Huntsville on September 4, 1861. Surrendered by General Joseph E. Johnston at Durham Station, Orange County, North Carolina, on April 26, 1865.

First Commander: Joseph Wheeler (Colonel)

Field Officers: Nicholas Davis (Colonel) (declined temporary assignment)

George R. Kimbrough (Lieutenant Colonel)
Samuel K. McSpadden (Major, Lieutenant Colonel, Colonel)
Solomon Palmer (Major)
James H. Savage (Major)
Edward D. Tracy (Lieutenant Colonel)

Assignments: Walker's Brigade, Department #1 (September-October 1861)
District of Alabama, Department of Alabama and West Florida (October 1861-January 1862)
Army of Mobile, Department of Alabama and West Florida (January-February 1862)
1st Brigade, 2nd Corps, 2nd Grand Division, Army of the Mississippi, Department #2 (March 1862)

Jackson's Brigade, Withers' Division, 2nd Corps, Army of the Mississippi, Department #2 (March-April 1862)

Gardner's Brigade, Withers' Division, 2nd Corps, Army of the Mississippi, Department #2 (April-June 1862)

Gardner's Brigade, Reserve Corps, Army of the Mississippi, Department #2 (June-July 1862)

Gardner's Brigade, Reserve Division, Army of the Mississippi, Department #2 (July-August 1862)

Gardner's Brigade, Withers' Division, Right Wing, Army of the Mississippi, Department #2 (August-November 1862)

Gardner's-Deas' Brigade, Withers'-Hindman's Division, 1st Corps, Army of Tennessee (November 1862-November 1863)

Deas' Brigade, Hindman's-Anderson's-Johnson's-D. H. Hill's Division, 2nd Corps, Army of Tennessee (November 1863-April 1865)

Pettus' Brigade, Stevenson's Division, 2nd Corps, Army of Tennessee (April 1865)

Battles: Shiloh (April 6-7, 1862)
Corinth Campaign (April-June 1862)
Murfreesboro (December 31, 1862-January 3, 1863)
Tullahoma Campaign (June 1863)
Chickamauga (September 19-20, 1863)
Chattanooga Siege (September-November 1863)
Chattanooga (November 23-25, 1863)
Atlanta Campaign (May-September 1864)
Dalton (May 5-11, 1864)
Resaca (May 14-15, 1864)
Cassville (May 19-22, 1864)
New Hope Church (May 25-June 4, 1864)
Kennesaw Mountain (June 27, 1864)
Peach Tree Creek (July 20, 1864)
Decatur Road (July 1864)
Ezra Church (July 28, 1864)
Jonesboro (August 31-September 1, 1864)
Atlanta Siege (July-September 1864)
Lovejoy's Station (September 2-5, 1864)
Franklin (November 30, 1864)
Nashville (December 15-16, 1864)
Carolinas Campaign (February-April 1865)
Bentonville (March 19-21, 1865)
Further Reading: *Roll and History of Company C, Nineteenth Alabama Regiment.*

143. ALABAMA 20TH INFANTRY REGIMENT

Organization: Organized at Montgomery on September 16, 1861. Regiment surrendered at Vicksburg, Mississippi, on July 4, 1863. Paroled there later in month. Consolidated with the 30th Infantry Regiment and designated as the 20th Infantry Regiment at Smithfield, North Carolina, on April 9, 1865.

First Commander: Isham W. Garrott (Lieutenant Colonel, Colonel)

Field Officers: John W. Davis (Major, Lieutenant Colonel)

James M. Dedman (Lieutenant Colonel, Colonel)

John G. Harris (Major)

Edmund W. Pettus (Major, Lieutenant Colonel, Colonel)

Alfred S. Pickering (Major)

Mitchell T. Porter (Major, Lieutenant Colonel)

Assignments: District of Alabama, Department of Alabama and West Florida (October 1861-January 1862)

Army of Mobile, Department of Alabama and West Florida (January-February 1862)

Barton's Brigade, Department of East Tennessee (May-June 1862)

Reynolds' Brigade, Stevenson's Division, Department of East Tennessee (June-October 1862)

Tracy's Brigade, McCown's Division, Department of East Tennessee (October-December 1862)

Tracy's Brigade, 2nd Military District, Department of Mississippi and East Louisiana (December 1862-January 1863)

Tracy's Brigade, Stevenson's Division, Department of Mississippi and East Louisiana (January-July 1863)

Pettus' Brigade, Stevenson's Division, 1st Corps, Army of Tennessee (November 1863-February 1864)

Pettus' Brigade, Stevenson's Division, 2nd Corps, Army of Tennessee (February 1864-April 1865)

Battles: Cumberland Gap (June 18, 1862)

Chickasaw Bayou (December 27-29, 1862)

Greenville Expedition (detachment) (April 2-25, 1863)

Vicksburg Campaign (May-July 1863)

Port Gibson (May 1, 1863)

Champion Hill (May 16, 1863)

Vicksburg Siege (May-July 1863)

Chattanooga Siege (September-November 1863)

Chattanooga (November 23-25, 1863)

Atlanta Campaign (May-September 1864)

Rocky Face Ridge (May 5-11, 1864)

New Hope Church (May 25-June 4, 1864)
Kennesaw Mountain (June 27, 1864)
Atlanta (July 22, 1864)
Atlanta Siege (July-September 1864)
Jonesboro (August 31-September 1, 1864)
Franklin (not engaged) (November 30, 1864)
Nashville (December 15-16, 1864)
Carolinas Campaign (February-April 1865)
Kinston (March 7-10, 1865)
Bentonville (March 19-21, 1865)
Further Reading: Williams, Hattie Eunice. *A Brief History of Company C, Twentieth Alabama Regiment of the War Between the States.*

144. ALABAMA 20TH INFANTRY REGIMENT CONSOLIDATED

Organization: Organized by the consolidation of the 20th and 30th Infantry Regiments at Smithfield, North Carolina, on April 9, 1865. Surrendered by General Joseph E. Johnston at Durham Station, Orange County, North Carolina, on April 26, 1865.
Field Officers: James K. Elliott (Lieutenant Colonel)
Assignment: Pettus' Brigade, Stevenson's Division, 2nd Corps, Army of Tennessee (April 1865)
Battle: Carolinas Campaign (February-April 1865)
Further Reading: Williams, Hattie Eunice. *A Brief History of Company C, Twentieth Alabama Regiment of the War Between the States.*

145. ALABAMA 21ST INFANTRY REGIMENT

Organization: Organized at Mobile during April to September 1861. Mustered into Confederate service for 12 months on October 13, 1861. Reorganized on May 8, 1862. Surrendered by Lieutenant Richard Taylor, commanding the Department of Alabama, Mississippi and East Louisiana, at Meridian, Mississippi, on May 4, 1865.
First Commander: James Crawford (Colonel)
Field Officers: Charles D. Anderson (Colonel)
Stewart W. Cayce (Lieutenant Colonel)
Andrew J. Ingersoll (Lieutenant Colonel)
Charles B. Johnston (Major)
Franklin J. McCoy (Major)
Charles S. Stewart (Major, Lieutenant Colonel)
Frederick Stewart (Major)
James M. Williams (Major, Lieutenant Colonel)

Assignments: Army of Mobile, Department of Alabama and West Florida (January-March 1862)

Gladden's Brigade, Withers' Division, 2nd Corps, Army of the Mississippi, Department #2 (March-April 1862)

Jackson's Brigade, Withers' Division, 2nd Corps, Army of the Mississippi, Department #2 (April-June 1862)

Jackson's Brigade, Reserve Corps, Army of the Mississippi, Department #2 (June-July 1862)

Jackson's Brigade, Reserve Division, Army of the Mississippi, Department #2 (July 1862)

District of the Gulf, Department #2 (July 1862-April 1863)

Slaughter's-Cantey's Brigade, Western Division, Department of the Gulf (1st Battalion) (April 1862-August 1863)

Powell's Brigade, Western Division, Department of the Gulf (2nd Battalion) (April 1862-August 1863)

Cantey's Brigade, Department of the Gulf (1st Battalion) (August-October 1863)

Powell's-Shoup's'-Higgins' Brigade, Department of the Gulf (2nd Battalion) (August 1863-January 1864)

Shoup's-Higgins' Brigade (1st Battalion) (November 1863-January 1864)

Page's Brigade, District of the Gulf, Department of Alabama, Mississippi and East Louisiana (April-August 1864)

Post of Mobile (Taylor's Command), District of the Gulf, Department of Alabama, Mississippi and East Louisiana (detachment) (October-December 1864)

Thomas' Brigade, District of the Gulf, Department of Alabama, Mississippi and East Louisiana (detachment) (March-April 1865)

Battles: Shiloh (April 6-7, 1862)

Corinth Campaign (April-June 1862)

Farmington (May 10, 1862)

Fort Gaines (six companies) (August 7-8, 1864)

Mobile (March 17-April 12, 1865)

Bay Minette Creek (March 26-27, 1865)

Spanish Fort (April 2-8, 1865)

Further Reading: Folmar, John Kent, ed. *From That Terrible Field: The Letters of James M. Williams, Twenty-First Alabama Infantry Volunteers.*

146. ALABAMA 22ND INFANTRY REGIMENT

Organization: Organized for the war at Montgomery on October 6, 1861. Field consolidation with the 25th Infantry Regiment during early 1863. Consolidated with the 25th, 39th and 50th Infantry Regiments at Smithfield, North Carolina, on April 9, 1865.

First Commander: Zachariah C. Deas (Colonel)

Field Officers: Edward H. Armistead (Major, Lieutenant Colonel)
Robert B. Armistead (Major)
Robert Donnell (Major)
Benjamin R. Hart (Major, Lieutenant Colonel, Colonel)
Jonathan C. Marrast (Lieutenant Colonel, Colonel)
Thomas M. Prince (Major)
Napoleon B. Rouse (Lieutenant Colonel)
Harry T. Toulmin (Major, Lieutenant Colonel, Colonel)
John Weedon (Major, Lieutenant Colonel)

Assignments: District of Alabama, Department of Alabama and West Florida (December 1861-January 1862)
Army of Mobile, Department of Alabama and West Florida (January-February 1862)
Adams' Brigade, 2nd Corps, 2nd Grand Division, Army of the Mississippi, Department #2 (March 1862)
Gladden's-Gardner's Brigade, Withers' Division, 2nd Corps, Army of the Mississippi, Department #2 (March-June 1862)
Gardner's Brigade, Reserve Corps, Army of the Mississippi, Department #2 (June-July 1862)
Gardner's Brigade, Reserve Division, Army of the Mississippi, Department #2 (July-August 1862)
Gardner's Brigade, Withers' Division, Right Wing, Army of the Mississippi, Department #2 (August-November 1862)
Gardner's-Deas' Brigade, Withers'-Hindman's Division, 1st Corps, Army of Tennessee (November 1862-November 1863)
Deas' Brigade, Hindman's-Anderson's-Johnson's-D. H. Hill's Division, 2nd Corps, Army of Tennessee (November 1863-April 1865)

Battles: Shiloh (April 6-7, 1862)
Corinth Campaign (April-June 1862)
Munfordville (September 17, 1862)
Murfreesboro (December 31, 1862-January 3, 1863)
Tullahoma Campaign (June 1863)
Chickamauga (September 19-20, 1863)
Chattanooga Siege (September-November 1863)
Chattanooga (November 23-25, 1863)
Atlanta Campaign (May-September 1864)
New Hope Church (May 25-June 4, 1864)
Peach Tree Creek (July 20, 1864)
Atlanta (July 22, 1864)
Ezra Church (July 28, 1864)
Atlanta Siege (July-September 1864)

Franklin (November 30, 1864)
Nashville (December 15-16, 1864)
Carolinas Campaign (February-April 1865)
Kinston (March 7-10, 1865)
Bentonville (March 19-21, 1865)

147. ALABAMA 22ND INFANTRY REGIMENT CONSOLIDATED

Organization: Organized by the consolidation of the 22nd, 25th, 39th and 50th Infantry Regiments at Smithfield, North Carolina, on April 9, 1865. Surrendered by General Joseph E. Johnston at Durham Station, Orange County, North Carolina, on April 26, 1865.
First Commander: Harry T. Toulmin (Colonel)
Assignment: Brantley Brigade, D. H. Hill's Division, 2nd Corps, Army of Tennessee (April 1865)

148. ALABAMA 23RD INFANTRY BATTALION SHARPSHOOTERS

Organization: Organized by the assignment of three companies from the 1st Infantry Battalion, Hilliard's Legion at Charleston, on November 25, 1863.
First Commander: Nicholas Stallworth (Major)
Assignments: Gracie's Brigade, Buckner's Division, Department of East Tennessee (December 1863-May 1864)
Gracie's Brigade, Department of Richmond (May-June 1864)
Gracie's Brigade, Johnson's Division, Department of North Carolina and Southern Virginia (July-October 1864)
Gracie's-Moody's Brigade, Johnson's Division, 4th Corps, Army of Northern Virginia (October 1864-April 1865)
Battles: Knoxville Siege (November 1863)
Dandridge (December 24, 1863)
Bean's Station (December 15, 1863)
Chester Station (May 10, 1864)
Drewry's Bluff (May 16, 1864)
Petersburg Siege (June 1864-April 1865)
The Crater (July 30, 1864)
Hatcher's Run (February 5-7, 1865)
White Oak Road (March 31, 1865)
Appomattox Court House (April 9, 1865)

149. ALABAMA 23RD INFANTRY REGIMENT

Organization: Organized at Montgomery on November 5, 1861. Regiment surrendered at Vicksburg, Mississippi, on July 4, 1863. Paroled there later in month. Declared exchanged in November 1863. Consolidated with the 31st and 46th Infantry Regiments and designated as the 23rd Infantry Regiment Consolidated at Smithfield, North Carolina, on April 9, 1865.

First Commander: Franklin K. Beck (Colonel)

Field Officers: Joseph B. Bibb (Lieutenant Colonel, Colonel)
James T. Hester (Major)
John J. Longmire (Major)
Francis McMurray (Major)
Felix Tait (Major)

Assignments: District of Alabama, Department of Alabama and West Florida (November 1861-January 1862)
Army of Mobile, Department of Alabama and West Florida (January-February 1862)
District of East Tennessee, Department #2 (March 1862)
Barton's Brigade, Department of East Tennessee (May-June 1862)
Taylor's Brigade, Stevenson's Division, Department of East Tennessee (June-October 1862)
Tracy's Brigade, McCown's Division, Department of East Tennessee (October-December 1862)
Tracy's Brigade, 2nd Military District, Department of Mississippi and East Louisiana (December 1862-January 1863)
Tracy's Brigade, Stevenson's Division, 2nd Military District, Department of Mississippi and East Louisiana (January-April 1863)
Tracy's-Garrott's-Lee's Brigade, Stevenson's Division, Department of Mississippi and East Louisiana (April-July 1863)
Pettus' Brigade, Stevenson's Division, 1st Corps, Army of Tennessee (November 1863-February 1864)
Pettus' Brigade, Stevenson's Division, 2nd Corps, Army of Tennessee (February 1864-April 1865)

Battles: Chickasaw Bayou (December 27-29, 1862)
Vicksburg Campaign (May-July 1863)
Port Gibson (May 1, 1863)
Champion Hill (May 16, 1863)
Vicksburg Siege (May-July 1863)
Chattanooga Siege (September-November 1863)
Chattanooga (November 23-25, 1863)
Atlanta Campaign (May-September 1864)
Rocky Face Ridge (May 5-11, 1864)
New Hope Church (May 25-June 4, 1864)
Atlanta (July 22, 1864)
Atlanta Siege (July-September 1864)
Jonesboro (August 31-September 1, 1864)

Franklin (not engaged) (November 30, 1864)
Nashville (December 15-16, 1864)
Carolinas Campaign (February-April 1865)
Bentonville (March 19-21, 1865)

150. ALABAMA 23RD INFANTRY REGIMENT CONSOLIDATED

Organization: Organized by the consolidation of the 23rd, 31st and 46th Infantry Regiments at Smithfield, North Carolina, on April 9, 1865.
First Commander: Joseph B. Bibb (Colonel)
Field Officers: Osceola Kyle (Lieutenant Colonel)
George W. Mattison (Major)
Assignment: Pettus' Brigade, Stevenson's Division, 2nd Corps, Army of Tennessee (April 1865)
Battle: Carolinas Campaign (February-April 1865)

151. ALABAMA 24TH INFANTRY REGIMENT

Organization: Organized at Mobile on October 15, 1861. Consolidated with the 28th and 34th Infantry Regiments and designated as the 24th Infantry Regiment Consolidated at Smithfield, North Carolina, on April 9, 1865.
First Commander: William A. Buck (Colonel)
Field Officers: Newton A. Davis (Major, Lieutenant Colonel, Colonel)
William B. Dennett (Lieutenant Colonel)
Junius J. Pierce (Major)
Benjamin F. Sawyer (Major, Lieutenant Colonel)
Assignments: District of Alabama, Department of Alabama and West Florida (October 1861-February 1862)
Army of Mobile, Department of Alabama and West Florida (January-April 1862)
Jackson's Brigade, Withers' Division, 2nd Corps, Army of the Mississippi, Department #2 (April-June 1862)
Jackson's Brigade, Reserve Corps, Army of the Mississippi, Department #2 (June-July 1862)
Jackson's Brigade, Reserve Division, Army of the Mississippi, Department #2 (July-August 1862)
Jackson's Brigade, Withers' Division, Right Wing, Army of the Mississippi, Department #2 (August-November 1862)
Duncan's Brigade, Withers' Division, Right Wing, Army of the Mississippi, Department #2 (November 1862)
Duncan's-Manigault's Brigade, Withers'-Hindman's Division, 1st Corps, Army of Tennessee (November 1862-November 1863)

Manigault's Brigade, Hindman's-Anderson's-Johnson's-D. H. Hill's Division, 2nd Corps, Army of Tennessee (November 1863-April 1865)
Battles: Shiloh (April 6-7, 1862)
Corinth Campaign (April-June 1862)
Murfreesboro (December 31, 1862-January 3, 1863)
Tullahoma Campaign (June 1863)
Chickamauga (September 19-20, 1863)
Chattanooga Siege (September-November 1863)
Chattanooga (November 23-25, 1863)
Atlanta Campaign (May-September 1864)
New Hope Church (May 25-June 4, 1864)
Ezra Church (July 28, 1864)
Atlanta Siege (July-September 1864)
Columbia (November 29, 1864)
Franklin (November 30, 1864)
Nashville (December 15-16, 1864)
Carolinas Campaign (February-April 1865)

152. ALABAMA 24TH INFANTRY REGIMENT CONSOLIDATED

Organization: Organized by the consolidation of the 24th, 28th and 34th Infantry Regiments Smithfield, North Carolina, on April 9, 1865.
First Commander: John C. Carter (Colonel)
Field Officers: Starke H. Oliver (Lieutenant Colonel)
P. G. Wood (Major)
Assignment: Sharp's Brigade, D. H. Hill's Division, 2nd Corps, Army of Tennessee (April 1865)
Battle: Carolinas Campaign (February-April 1865)

153. ALABAMA 25TH INFANTRY REGIMENT

Organization: Organized by the consolidation of the 1st (Loomis') and 6th (McClellan's) Infantry Battalions at Mobile on January 8, 1862. Field consolidation with the 22nd Infantry Regiment in early 1863. Consolidated with the 22nd, 39th and 50th Infantry Regiments at Smithfield, North Carolina, on April 9, 1865.
First Commander: John Q. Loomis (Colonel)
Field Officers: Daniel E. Huger (Major)
George D. Johnston (Major, Lieutenant Colonel, Colonel)
William B. McClellan (Lieutenant Colonel)
Assignments: Army of Mobile, Department of Alabama and West Florida (January-February 1862)

Wheeler's Brigade, 2nd Corps, 2nd Grand Division, Army of the Mississippi, Department #2 (February-March 1862)

Gladden's-Gardner's Brigade, Withers' Division, 2nd Corps, Army of the Mississippi, Department #2 (March-June 1862)

Gardner's Brigade, Reserve Corps, Army of the Mississippi, Department #2 (June-July 1862)

Gardner's Brigade, Reserve Division, Army of the Mississippi, Department #2 (July-August 1862)

Gardner's Brigade, Withers' Division, Right Wing, Army of the Mississippi, Department #2 (August-November 1862)

Gardner's-Deas' Brigade, Withers'-Hindman's Division, 1st Corps, Army of Tennessee (November 1862-November 1863)

Deas' Brigade, Hindman's-Anderson's-Johnson's-D. H. Hill's Division, 2nd Corps, Army of Tennessee (November 1863-April 1865)

Battles: Shiloh (April 6-7, 1862)
Corinth Campaign (April-June 1862)
Murfreesboro (December 31, 1862-January 3, 1863)
Tullahoma Campaign (June 1863)
Chickamauga (September 19-20, 1863)
Chattanooga Siege (September-November 1863)
Chattanooga (November 23-25, 1863)
Atlanta Campaign (May-September 1864)
New Hope Church (May 25-June 4, 1864)
Peach Tree Creek (July 20, 1864)
Atlanta (July 22, 1864)
Ezra Church (July 28, 1864)
Atlanta Siege (July-September 1864)
Franklin (November 30, 1864)
Nashville (December 15-16, 1864)
Carolinas Campaign (February-April 1865)
Kinston (March 7-10, 1865)
Bentonville (March 19-21, 1865)

154. ALABAMA 26TH INFANTRY REGIMENT

Organization: Organized by the increasing of the 3rd Infantry Battalion to a regiment on March 27, 1862. Merged into the 1st Infantry Regiment Consolidated in April 1865.

First Commander: William R. Smith (Colonel)
Field Officers: David F. Bryan (Major)
John S. Garvin (Lieutenant Colonel)
William H. Hunt (Lieutenant Colonel)

Edward A. O'Neal (Colonel)
Raymond D. Redden (Major)
William C. Reeder (Major, Lieutenant Colonel)

Assignments: Rains' Brigade, D. H. Hill's Division, Army of Northern Virginia (April-June 1862)

Rodes' Brigade, D. H. Hill's Division, Army of Northern Virginia (June-September 1862)

Rodes'-O'Neal's-Battle's Brigade, D. H. Hill's Division, 2nd Corps, Army of Northern Virginia (September 1862-February 1864)

Duty at Richmond, Virginia, and guards for prisoners of war en route to Andersonville, Georgia (February-June 1864)

Cantey's Brigade, Walthall's Division, Army of Mississippi (June-July 1864)

Cantey's-Shelley's Brigade, Walthall's Division, 3rd Corps, Army of Tennessee (July-December 1864)

Battles: Yorktown Siege (April-May 1862)
Williamsburg (May 5, 1862)
Seven Pines (May 31-June 1, 1862)
Seven Days Battles (June 25-July 1, 1862)
Gaines' Mill (June 27, 1862)
Malvern Hill (July 1, 1862)
South Mountain (September 14, 1862)
Antietam (September 17, 1862)
Fredericksburg (December 13, 1862)
Chancellorsville (May 1-4, 1863)
Gettysburg (July 1-3, 1863)
Manassas Gap (July 23, 1863)
Kelly's Ford (November 7, 1863)
Bristoe Campaign (October 1863)
Mine Run Campaign (November-December 1863)
Atlanta Campaign (May-September 1864)
Peach Tree Creek (July 20, 1864)
Ezra Church (July 28, 1864)
Atlanta Siege (July-September 1864)
Jonesboro (August 31-September 1, 1864)
Franklin (November 30, 1864)
Nashville (December 15-16, 1864)
Carolinas Campaign (February-April 1865)

155. ALABAMA 26TH (COLTART'S) INFANTRY REGIMENT

See: ALABAMA 50TH INFANTRY REGIMENT

156. ALABAMA 27TH INFANTRY REGIMENT

Organization: Organized by the increase of Foster's Infantry Battalion to a regiment at Fort Heiman on January 28, 1862. Surrendered at Fort Donelson on February 16, 1862. Survivors attached to the 33rd Mississippi Infantry Regiment. Exchanged at Vicksburg, Mississippi, on September 4, 1862. Reorganized at Jackson, Mississippi, in October 1862. Field consolidation with the 31st (Hale's) Infantry Regiment and the 6th (Norwood's) Infantry Battalion from October 1862 to January 1863. Field consolidation with the 35th and 49th Infantry Regiments from July 1864 to April 9, 1865.

First Commander: Adolphus A. Hugh (Colonel)

Field Officers: James Jackson (Lieutenant Colonel, Colonel)
Edward McAlexander (Major, Lieutenant Colonel)
R. G. Wright (Major)

Assignments: Heiman's Brigade, Fort Henry, Department #2 (December 1861-February 1862)

Heiman's Brigade, Johnson's Division, Fort Donelson, Department #2 (February 1862)

(———— Brigade), Maury's Division, Army of West Tennessee, Department of Mississippi and East Louisiana (October 1862)

Beall's Brigade, 3rd Military District, Department of Mississippi and East Louisiana (November 1862-February 1863)

Buford's Brigade, 3rd Military District, Department of Mississippi and East Louisiana (March-April 1863)

Buford's Brigade, Loring's Division, Department of Mississippi and East Louisiana (May 1863)

Buford's Brigade, Loring's Division, Department of the West (May-July 1863)

Buford's Brigade, Loring's Division, Department of Mississippi and East Louisiana (July 1863-January 1864)

Buford's Brigade, Loring's Division, Department of Alabama, Mississippi and East Louisiana (January-February 1864)

District of Northern Alabama, Department of Alabama, Mississippi and East Louisiana (February-May 1864)

Scott's Brigade, Loring's Division, Army of Mississippi (May-July 1864)

Scott's Brigade, Loring's Division, 3rd Corps, Army of Tennessee (July 1864-April 1865)

Battles: Fort Henry (February 6, 1862)
Fort Donelson (February 12-16, 1862)
Vicksburg Campaign (May-July 1863)
Champion Hill (May 16, 1863)
Jackson Siege (July 1863)
Meridian Campaign (February-March 1864)

Morton (February 8, 1864)
Chunky Mountain (February 12, 1864)
Moulton (March 21, 1864)
near Florence, Alabama (April 12, 1864)
Atlanta Campaign (May-September 1864)
Resaca (May 14-15, 1864)
New Hope Church (May 25-June 4, 1864)
Kennesaw Mountain (June 27, 1864)
Peach Tree Creek (July 20, 1864)
Ezra Church (July 28, 1864)
Atlanta Siege (July-September 1864)
Jonesboro (August 31-September 1, 1864)
Ackworth (October 4, 1864)
Franklin (November 30, 1864)
Nashville (December 15-16, 1864)
Carolinas Campaign (February-April 1865)
Kinston (March 7-10, 1865)
Bentonville (March 19-21, 1865)
Further Reading: Barnard, Harry Vollie. Tattered Volunteers, the Twenty-seventh Alabama Infantry Regiment.

157. ALABAMA 27TH INFANTRY REGIMENT CONSOLIDATED

Organization: Organized by the consolidation of the 27th, 35th, 49th, 55th and 57th Infantry Regiments at Smithfield, North Carolina, on April 9, 1865. Surrendered by General Joseph E. Johnston at Durham Station, Orange County, North Carolina, on April 26, 1865.
First Commander: Edward McAlexander (Colonel)
Assignment: Shelley's Brigade, Loring's Division, 3rd Corps, Army of Tennessee (April 1865)
Battle: Carolinas Campaign (February-April 1865)

158. ALABAMA 28TH INFANTRY REGIMENT

Organization: Organized for three years at Shelby Springs in March 1862. Field consolidation with the 34th Infantry Regiment in early 1863. Consolidated with the 24th and 34th Infantry Regiments and designated as the 24th Infantry Regiment Consolidated Smithfield, North Carolina, on April 9, 1865.
First Commander: Jonathan W. Frazer (Colonel)
Field Officers: William L. Butler (Major, Lieutenant Colonel)
Thomas W. W. Davies (Major, Lieutenant Colonel)
Jonathan C. Reid (Lieutenant Colonel, Colonel)

Assignments: Trapier's-Manigault's Brigade, Withers' Division, 2nd Corps, Army of the Mississippi, Department #2 (April-June 1862)
Manigault's Brigade, Reserve Corps, Army of the Mississippi, Department #2 (June-July 1862)
Manigault's Brigade, Reserve Division, Army of the Mississippi, Department #2 (July-August 1862)
Manigault's Brigade, Withers' Division, Right Wing, Army of the Mississippi, Department #2 (August-November 1862)
Manigault's Brigade, Withers'-Hindman's Division, 1st Corps, Army of Tennessee (November 1862-November 1863)
Manigault's Brigade, Hindman's-Anderson's-Johnson's-D. H. Hill's Division, 2nd Corps, Army of Tennessee (November 1863-April 1865)
Battles: Corinth Campaign (April-June 1862)
Munfordville (September 17, 1862)
Murfreesboro (December 31, 1862-January 3, 1863)
Tullahoma Campaign (June 1863)
Chickamauga (September 19-20, 1863)
Chattanooga Siege (September-November 1863)
Chattanooga (November 23-25, 1863)
Atlanta Campaign (May-September 1864)
New Hope Church (May 25-June 4, 1864)
Ezra Church (July 28, 1864)
Atlanta Siege (July-September 1864)
Columbia (November 29, 1864)
Franklin (November 30, 1864)
Nashville (December 15-16, 1864)
Carolinas Campaign (February-April 1865)

159. ALABAMA 29TH INFANTRY REGIMENT

Organization: Organized by the addition of two companies to the 4th (Conoley's) Infantry Battalion on March 10, 1862. Field consolidation with the 1st and 17th Infantry Regiments from early 1865 to April 9, 1865. Surrendered by General Joseph E. Johnston at Durham Station, Orange County, North Carolina, on April 26, 1865.
First Commander: Jonathan R. F. Tattnall (Colonel)
Field Officers: John F. Conoley (Lieutenant Colonel, Colonel)
Benjamin Morris (Major, Lieutenant Colonel)
Henry B. Turner (Major)
Assignments: Department of Alabama and West Florida (April-July 1862)
District of the Gulf, Department #2 (July 1862-April 1863)
Eastern Division, Department of the Gulf (April 1863)

Cantey's Brigade, Western Division, Department of the Gulf (August 1863-
April 1864)
Cantey's Brigade, Army of Tennessee (April-May 1864)
Cantey's Brigade, Army of Mississippi (May 1864)
Cantey's Brigade, French's Division, Army of Mississippi (May 1864)
Cantey's Brigade, Cantey's-Walthall's Division, Army of Mississippi (June-July
1864)
Cantey's-Shelley's Brigade, Walthall's Division, 3rd Corps, Army of Tennessee
(July-December 1864)
Quarles' Brigade, Walthall's Division, 3rd Corps, Army of Tennessee (March-
April 1865)
Lowry's Brigade, Loring's Division, 3rd Corps, Army of Tennessee (April 1865)
Battles: Atlanta Campaign (May-September 1864)
Resaca (May 14-15, 1864)
New Hope Church (May 25-June 4, 1864)
Peach Tree Creek (July 20, 1864)
Ezra Church (July 28, 1864)
Atlanta Siege (July-September 1864)
Jonesboro (August 31-September 1, 1864)
Franklin (November 30, 1864)
Nashville (December 15-16, 1864)
Carolinas Campaign (February-April 1865)
Kinston (March 7-10, 1865)
Bentonville (March 19-21, 1865)

160. ALABAMA 30TH INFANTRY REGIMENT

Organization: Organized at Talladega in April 1862. Regiment surrendered
at Vicksburg, Mississippi, on July 4, 1863. Paroled there later in month.
Declared exchanged in November 1863. Consolidated with the 20th Infantry
Regiment and designated as the 20th Infantry Regiment Consolidated at
Smithfield, North Carolina, on April 9, 1865.
First Commander: Charles M. Shelley (Colonel)
Field Officers: Taul Bradford (Lieutenant Colonel)
William H. Burr (Major)
James K. Elliott (Major, Lieutenant Colonel)
John C. Francis (Lieutenant Colonel)
Thomas H. Patterson (Major, Lieutenant Colonel)
William C. Patterson (Major, Lieutenant Colonel)
John B. Smith (Major)
Assignments: Stevenson's Brigade, Department of East Tennessee (May-June
1862)

Barton's Brigade, Stevenson's Division, Department of East Tennessee (June-December 1862)

Tracy's Brigade, 2nd Military District, Department of Mississippi and East Louisiana (December 1862-January 1863)

Tracy's Brigade, Stevenson's Division, 2nd Military District, Department of Mississippi and East Louisiana (January-April 1863)

Tracy's-Garrott's-Lee's Brigade, Stevenson's Division, Department of Mississippi and East Louisiana (April-July 1863)

Pettus' Brigade, Stevenson's Division, 1st Corps, Army of Tennessee (November 1863-February 1864)

Pettus' Brigade, Stevenson's Division, 2nd Corps, Army of Tennessee (February 1864-April 1865)

Battles: Cumberland Gap (June 18, 1862)
Chickasaw Bayou (December 27-29, 1862)
Vicksburg Campaign (May-July 1863)
Port Gibson (May 1, 1863)
Champion Hill (May 16, 1863)
Vicksburg Siege (May-July 1863)
Chattanooga Siege (September-November 1863)
Chattanooga (November 23-25, 1863)
Atlanta Campaign (May-September 1864)
New Hope Church (May 25-June 4, 1864)
Atlanta (July 22, 1864)
Atlanta Siege (July-September 1864)
Franklin (not engaged) (November 30, 1864)
Nashville (December 15-16, 1864)
Carolinas Campaign (February-April 1865)
Kinston (March 7-10, 1865)
Bentonville (March 19-21, 1865)

161. ALABAMA 31ST INFANTRY REGIMENT

Organization: Organized at Talladega on March 16, 1862. Regiment surrendered at Vicksburg, Mississippi, on July 4, 1863. Paroled there later in month. Declared exchanged in November 1863. Consolidated with the 23rd and 46th Infantry Regiments and designated as the 23rd Infantry Regiment Consolidated at Smithfield, North Carolina, on April 9, 1865.

First Commander: Daniel R. Hundley (Colonel)

Field Officers: Thomas M. Arrington (Lieutenant Colonel)
George W. Mattison (Major)

Assignments: Unattached, Department of East Tennessee (May-June 1862)

Barton's Brigade, Stevenson's Division, Department of East Tennessee (June-December 1862)

Tracy's Brigade, 2nd Military District, Department of Mississippi and East Louisiana (December 1862-January 1863)

Tracy's Brigade, Stevenson's Division, 2nd Military District, Department of Mississippi and East Louisiana (January-April 1863)

Tracy's-Garrott's-Lee's Brigade, Stevenson's Division, Department of Mississippi and East Louisiana (April-July 1863)

Pettus Brigade, Stevenson's Division, 1st Corps, Army of Tennessee (November 1863-February 1864)

Pettus' Brigade, Stevenson's Division, 2nd Corps, Army of Tennessee (February 1864-April 1865)

Battles: Cumberland Gap (June 18, 1862)
Vicksburg Bombardments (May 18-27, 1862)
Chickasaw Bayou (December 27-29, 1862)
Vicksburg Campaign (May-July 1863)
Port Gibson (May 1, 1863)
Champion Hill (May 16, 1863)
Vicksburg Siege (May-July 1863)
Chattanooga Siege (September-November 1863)
Chattanooga (November 23-25, 1863)
Atlanta Campaign (May-September 1864)
New Hope Church (May 25-June 4, 1864)
Big Shanty (June 15, 1864)
Atlanta (July 22, 1864)
Atlanta Siege (July-September 1864)
Jonesboro (August 31-September 1, 1864)
Franklin (not engaged) (November 30, 1864)
Nashville (December 15-16, 1864)
Carolinas Campaign (February-April 1865)
Bentonville (March 19-21, 1865)
Further Reading: Hundley, Daniel Robinson. *Prison Echoes of the Great Rebellion* (POW records only).

162.   ALABAMA 31ST (HALE'S) INFANTRY REGIMENT
See: ALABAMA 49TH INFANTRY REGIMENT

163.   ALABAMA 32ND INFANTRY REGIMENT
Organization: Organized for three years at Mobile on April 18, 1862. Field consolidation with the 58th Infantry Regiment from November 24, 1863, to May 4, 1865. Surrendered by Lieutenant Richard Taylor, commanding the Department of

Alabama, Mississippi and East Louisiana, at Meridian, Mississippi, on May 4, 1865.

First Commander: Alexander McKinstry (Colonel)

Field Officers: Thomas P. Ashe (Major)
Thomas E. Easton (Major)
John C. Kimbrell (Major)
Henry Maury (Lieutenant Colonel)

Assignments: Jackson's Brigade, Withers' Division, Right Wing, Army of the Mississippi, Department #2 (August 1862)
Palmer's Brigade, Army of Middle Tennessee, Department #2 (October-November 1862)
Palmer's Brigade, Breckinridge's Division, 1st Corps, Army of Tennessee (November-December 1862)
Adams' Brigade, Breckinridge's Division, 2nd Corps, Army of Tennessee (December 1862-May 1863)
Adams' Brigade, Breckinridge's Division, Department of the West (May-July 1863)
Adams' Brigade, Breckinridge's Division, Department of Mississippi and East Louisiana (July-August 1863)
Adams' Brigade, Breckinridge's Division, 2nd Corps, Army of Tennessee (August-November 1863)
Clayton's-Holtzclaw's Brigade, Stewart's-Clayton's Division, 2nd Corps, Army of Tennessee (November 1863-January 1865)
Holtzclaw's Brigade, District of the Gulf, Department of Alabama, Mississippi and East Louisiana (January-April 1865)
Holtzclaw's Brigade, Department of Alabama, Mississippi and East Louisiana (April-May 1865)

Battles: Bridgeport and Battle Creek (August 27, 1862)
Murfreesboro (December 31, 1862-January 3, 1863)
Jackson Siege (July 1863)
Chickamauga (September 19-20, 1863)
Chattanooga Siege (September-November 1863)
Chattanooga (November 23-25, 1863)
Atlanta Campaign (May-September 1864)
New Hope Church (May 25-June 4, 1864)
Atlanta (July 22, 1864)
Ezra Church (July 28, 1864)
Atlanta Siege (July-September 1864)
Columbia (November 29, 1864)
Franklin (November 30, 1864)
Nashville (December 15-16, 1864)
Mobile (March 17-April 12, 1865)

Spanish Fort (April 2-8, 1865)

164. ALABAMA 33RD INFANTRY REGIMENT

Organization: Organized at Pensacola, Florida, on April 23, 1862. 18th Infantry Battalion merged into this regiment in the fall of 1863. Field consolidation with the 16th and 45th Infantry Regiments from the fall of 1864 to April 1865. Consolidated with the 1st (apparently), 16th and 45th Infantry Regiments at Smithfield, North Carolina, on April 8, 1865.

First Commander: Samuel Adams (Colonel)

Field Officers: Robert F. Crittenden (Major, Lieutenant Colonel, Colonel)
James H. Dunklin (Major, Lieutenant Colonel)
Daniel H. Horn (Lieutenant Colonel)

Assignments: Hawthorn's Brigade, 3rd Corps, Army of the Mississippi, Department #2 (June-July 1862)
Hawthorn's Brigade, Hardee's Division, Army of the Mississippi, Department #2 (July 1862)
Wood's Brigade, Hardee's Division, Army of the Mississippi, Department #2 (August 1862)
Wood's Brigade, Buckner's Division, Left Wing, Army of the Mississippi, Department #2 (August-November 1862)
Wood's-Lowrey's Brigade, Buckner's-Cleburne's Division, 2nd Corps, Army of Tennessee (November 1862-November 1863)
Lowrey's Brigade, Cleburne's Division, 1st Corps, Army of Tennessee (November 1863-April 1865)

Battles: Munfordville (September 17, 1862)
Perryville (October 8, 1862)
Murfreesboro (December 31, 1862-January 3, 1863)
Chickamauga (September 19-20, 1863)
Chattanooga Siege (September-November 1863)
Chattanooga (November 23-25, 1863)
Ringgold Gap (November 27, 1863)
Atlanta Campaign (May-September 1864)
New Hope Church (May 25-June 4, 1864)
Kennesaw Mountain (June 27, 1864)
Atlanta (July 22, 1864)
Ezra Church (July 28, 1864)
Atlanta Siege (July-September 1864)
Jonesboro (August 31-September 1, 1864)
Franklin (November 30, 1864)
Nashville (December 15-16, 1864)
Carolinas Campaign (February-April 1865)

165. ALABAMA 34TH INFANTRY REGIMENT

Organization: Organized at Loachapoka on April 15, 1862. Field consolidation
with the 28th Infantry Regiment in early 1863.
First Commander: Julius C. B. Mitchell (Colonel)
Field Officers: John C. Carter (Lieutenant Colonel)
James W. Echols (Lieutenant Colonel)
Henry R. McCoy (Major)
John N. Slaughter (Major)
Assignments: Manigault's Brigade, Reserve Corps, Army of the Mississippi,
   Department #2 (June-July 1862)
Manigault's Brigade, Reserve Division, Army of the Mississippi, Department #2
   (July-August 1862)
Manigault's Brigade, Withers' Division, Right Wing, Army of the Mississippi,
   Department #2 (August-November 1862)
Manigault's Brigade, Withers'-Hindman's Division, 1st Corps, Army of Tennessee
   (November 1862-November 1863)
Manigault's Brigade, Hindman's-Anderson's-Johnson's-D. H. Hill's Division, 2nd
   Corps, Army of Tennessee (November 1863-April 1865)
Battles: Murfreesboro (December 31, 1862-January 3, 1863)
Tullahoma Campaign (June 1863)
Chickamauga (September 19-20, 1863)
Chattanooga Siege (September-November 1863)
Chattanooga (November 23-25, 1863)
Atlanta Campaign (May-September 1864)
New Hope Church (May 25-June 4, 1864)
Ezra Church (July 28, 1864)
Atlanta Siege (July-September 1864)
Columbia (November 29, 1864)
Franklin (November 30, 1864)
Nashville (December 15-16, 1864)
Further Reading: Maxwell, James Robert. *Autobiography of James Robert Maxwell
of Tuscaloosa, Alabama.*

166. ALABAMA 35TH INFANTRY REGIMENT

Organization: Organized at La Grange on March 12, 1862. Mustered in on April
15, 1862. Field consolidation with the 27th and 49th Infantry Regiments from July
1864 to April 9, 1865. Consolidated with the 27th, 49th, 55th and 57th Infantry
Regiments and designated as the 27th Infantry Regiment Consolidated at
Smithfield, North Carolina, on April 9, 1865.
First Commander: James W. Robertson (Colonel)
Field Officers: Alva E. Ashford (Major)

Edward Goodwin (Lieutenant Colonel, Colonel)

Samuel S. Ives (Major, Lieutenant Colonel, Colonel)

Assignments: Preston's Brigade, Reserve Corps, Army of the Mississippi, Department #2 (May-June 1862)

Preston's Brigade, Breckinridge's Command, District of the Mississippi, Department #2 (June-July 1862)

Thompson's-Robertson's Brigade, Ruggles' Division, Breckinridge's Command, District of the Mississippi, Department #2 (July-August 1862)

Rust's Brigade, Lovell's Division, District of the Mississippi, Department #2 (October 1862)

Rust's Brigade, Lovell's Division, Van Dorn's Corps, Price's Corps, Army of West Tennessee, Department of Mississippi and East Louisiana (October-December 1862)

(———— Brigade), Rust's Division, 1st Corps, Army of North Mississippi, Department of Mississippi and East Louisiana (December 1862-January 1863)

Rust's Brigade, Loring's Division, Army of North Mississippi, Department of Mississippi and East Louisiana (January 1863)

Rust's Brigade, 3rd Military District, Department of Mississipp: and East Louisiana (January-April 1863)

Buford's Brigade, Loring's Division, Department of Mississippi and East Louisiana (April-May 1863)

Buford's Brigade, Loring's Division, Department of the West (May-July 1863)

Buford's Brigade, Loring's Division, Department of Mississippi and East Louisiana (July 1863-January 1864)

Buford's Brigade, Loring's Division, Department of Alabama, Mississippi and East Louisiana (January-February 1864)

District of Northern Alabama, Department of Alabama, Mississippi and East Louisiana (February-May 1864)

Scott's Brigade, Loring's Division, Army of Mississippi (May-July 1864)

Scott's Brigade, Loring's Division, 3rd Corps, Army of Tennessee (July 1864-April 1865)

Battles: Corinth Campaign (April-June 1862)

Vicksburg Bombardments (May 18-27, 1862)

Baton Rouge (August 5, 1862)

Corinth (October 3-4, 1862)

Vicksburg Campaign (May-July 1863)

Champion Hill (May 16, 1863)

Jackson Siege (July 1863)

Meridian Campaign (February-March 1864)

Moulton (March 21, 1864)

near Florence, Alabama (April 12, 1864)

Atlanta Campaign (May-September 1864)
New Hope Church (May 25-June 4, 1864)
Peach Tree Creek (July 20, 1864)
Ezra Church (July 28, 1864)
Atlanta Siege (July-September 1864)
Jonesboro (August 31-September 1, 1864)
Franklin (November 30, 1864)
Nashville (December 15-16, 1864)
Carolinas Campaign (February-April 1865)
Further Reading: Goodloe, Albert Theodore. *Confederate Echoes, A Voice From the South in the Days of Secession and of the Southern Confederacy.*

167. ALABAMA 36TH INFANTRY REGIMENT

Organization: Organized at Mount Vernon on May 12, 1862. Surrendered by Lieutenant Richard Taylor, commanding the Department of Alabama, Mississippi and East Louisiana, at Meridian, Mississippi, on May 4, 1865.
First Commander: Robert H. Smith (Colonel)
Field Officers: Charles S. Henagan (Major)
Thomas H. Herndon (Major, Lieutenant Colonel, Colonel)
Louis T. Woodruff (Lieutenant Colonel, Colonel)
Assignments: Army of Mobile, Department of Alabama and West Florida (May-June 1862)
Army of Mobile, District of the Gulf, Department #2 (July 1862-April 1863)
Cumming's Brigade, Western Division, Department of the Gulf (April 1863)
Clayton's Brigade, Stewart's Division, 2nd Corps, Army of Tennessee (April-September 1863)
Clayton's Brigade, Stewart's Division, Buckner's Corps, Army of Tennessee (September-October 1863)
Clayton's-Holtzclaw's Brigade, Stewart's-Clayton's Division, 2nd Corps, Army of Tennessee (October 1863-January 1865)
Holtzclaw's Brigade, District of the Gulf, Department of Alabama, Mississippi and East Louisiana (January-April 1865)
Holtzclaw's Brigade, Department of Alabama, Mississippi and East Louisiana (April-May 1865)
Battles: Chickamauga (September 19-20, 1863)
Chattanooga Siege (September-November 1863)
Chattanooga (November 23-25, 1863)
Crow Valley (February 24, 1864)
Atlanta Campaign (May-September 1864)
Rocky Face Ridge (May 5-11, 1864)
Resaca (May 14-15, 1864)

New Hope Church (May 25-June 4, 1864)
Atlanta (July 22, 1864)
Ezra Church (July 28, 1864)
Atlanta Siege (July-September 1864)
Jonesboro (August 31-September 1, 1864)
Franklin (not engaged) (November 30, 1864)
Nashville (December 15-16, 1864)
Mobile (March 17-April 12, 1865)
Spanish Fort (April 2-8, 1865)

168. ALABAMA 37TH INFANTRY REGIMENT

Organization: Organized and mustered into Confederate service for three years or the war at Auburn on May 13, 1862. Regiment surrendered at Vicksburg, Mississippi, on July 4, 1863. Paroled there later in month. Declared exchanged in November 1863. Field consolidation with the 40th and 42nd Infantry Regiments from November 1864 to early 1865. Consolidated with the 42nd and 54th Infantry Regiments and designated as the 37th Infantry Regiment Consolidated at Smithfield, North Carolina, on April 9, 1865.
First Commander: James F. Dowdell (Colonel)
Field Officers: John P. W. Amerine (Major)
Alexander A. Greene (Lieutenant Colonel)
William F. Slaton (Major)

Assignments: Martin's Brigade, Little's-Hébert's Division, Price's Corps, Army of West Tennessee, Department of Mississippi and East Louisiana (September-October 1862)
Moore's Brigade, Maury's Division, Price's Corps, Army of West Tennessee, Department of Mississippi and East Louisiana (October-December 1862)
(——— Brigade), Provisional Division, 2nd Military District, Department of Mississippi and East Louisiana (December 1862-January 1863)
Moore's Brigade, Maury's-Forney's Division, 2nd Military District, Department of Mississippi and East Louisiana (January-April 1863)
Moore's Brigade, Forney's Division, Department of Mississippi and East Louisiana (April-July 1863)
Moore's Brigade, Cheatham's Division, 1st Corps, Army of Tennessee (November 1863-February 1864)
Moore's-Baker's Brigade, Stewart's-Clayton's Division, 2nd Corps, Army of Tennessee (February-September 1864)
Baker's Brigade, District of the Gulf, Department of Alabama, Mississippi and East Louisiana (September-October 1864)
Baker's Brigade, Liddell's Division, District of the Gulf, Department of Alabama, Mississippi and East Louisiana (October 1864-January 1865)

Baker's Brigade, Clayton's Division, 2nd Corps, Army of Tennessee (January-April 1865)
Battles: Iuka (September 19, 1862)
Corinth (October 3-4, 1862)
Chickasaw Bayou (December 27-29, 1862)
vs. Yazoo Pass Expedition (February 3-10, 1863)
Vicksburg Campaign (May-July 1863)
Port Gibson (May 1, 1863)
Champion Hill (May 16, 1863)
Vicksburg Siege (May-July 1863)
Chattanooga Siege (September-November 1863)
Chattanooga (November 23-25, 1863)
Atlanta Campaign (May-September 1864)
Rocky Face Ridge (May 5-11, 1864)
Resaca (May 14-15, 1864)
New Hope Church (May 25-June 4, 1864)
Atlanta (July 22, 1864)
Ezra Church (July 28, 1864)
Atlanta Siege (July-September 1864)
Carolinas Campaign (February-April 1865)

169.   ALABAMA 37TH INFANTRY REGIMENT CONSOLIDATED
Organization: Organized by the consolidation of the 37th, 42nd and 54th Infantry Regiments at Smithfield, North Carolina, on April 9, 1865. Surrendered by General Joseph E. Johnston at Durham Station, Orange County, North Carolina, on April 26, 1865.
First Commander: John A. Minter (Colonel)
Field Officer: William D. McNeill (Lieutenant Colonel)
Assignment: Brantley's Brigade, D .H. Hill's Division, 2nd Corps, Army of Tennessee (April 1865)
Battle: Carolinas Campaign (February-April 1865)

170.   ALABAMA 38TH INFANTRY REGIMENT
Organization: Organized and mustered into Confederate service for three years or the war at Mobile on May 15, 1862. Surrendered by Lieutenant Richard Taylor, commanding the Department of Alabama, Mississippi and East Louisiana, at Meridian, Mississippi, on May 4, 1865.
First Commander: Charles T. Ketchum (Colonel)
Field Officers: William J. Hearin (Major, Lieutenant Colonel)
Origen S. Jewett (Major)
Augustus R. Lankford (Lieutenant Colonel, Colonel)

Assignments: Army of Mobile, Department of Alabama and West Florida
(May-June 1862)
Army of Mobile, District of the Gulf, Department #2 (July 1862-April 1863)
Cumming's Brigade, Western Division, Department of the Gulf (April 1863)
Clayton's Brigade, Stewart's Division, 2nd Corps, Army of Tennessee (April-
September 1863)
Clayton's Brigade, Stewart's Division, Buckner's Corps, Army of Tennessee
(September-October 1863)
Clayton's-Holtzclaw's Brigade, Stewart's-Clayton's Division, 2nd Corps, Army
of Tennessee (October 1863-January 1865)
Holtzclaw's Brigade, District of the Gulf, Department of Alabama, Mississippi
and East Louisiana (January-April 1865)
Holtzclaw's Brigade, Department of Alabama, Mississippi and East Louisiana
(April-May 1865)
Battles: Tullahoma Campaign (June 1863)
Chickamauga (September 19-20, 1863)
Chattanooga Siege (September-November 1863)
Chattanooga (November 23-25, 1863)
Atlanta Campaign (May-September 1864)
Rocky Face Ridge (May 5-11, 1864)
Resaca (May 14-15, 1864)
New Hope Church (May 25-June 4, 1864)
Peach Tree Creek (July 20, 1864)
Atlanta (July 22, 1864)
Ezra Church (July 28, 1864)
Atlanta Siege (July-September 1864)
Franklin (not engaged) (November 30, 1864)
Nashville (December 15-16, 1864)
Mobile (March 17-April 12, 1865)

171. ALABAMA 39TH INFANTRY REGIMENT

Organization: Organized at Opelika on May 15, 1862. Field consolidation
with the 26th (Coltart's) Infantry Regiment in early 1863. Consolidated with
the 22nd, 25th and 50th Infantry Regiments and designated as the 22nd
Infantry Regiment Consolidated at Smithfield, North Carolina, on April 9,
1865.
First Commander: Henry D. Clayton (Colonel)
Field Officers: Whitfield Clark (Major, Lieutenant Colonel, Colonel)
William C. Clifton (Lieutenant Colonel, Colonel)
James T. Flewellen (Lieutenant Colonel)

Lemuel Hargrove (Major, Lieutenant Colonel)
Colin McSwean (Major)
Drewry H. Smith (Major)

Assignments: Gardner's Brigade, Withers' Division, 2nd Corps, Army of the
Mississippi, Department #2 (June 1862)
Gardner's Brigade, Reserve Corps, Army of the Mississippi, Department #2
(June-July 1862)
Gardner's Brigade, Reserve Division, Army of the Mississippi, Department #2
(July-August 1862)
Gardner's Brigade, Withers' Division, Right Wing, Army of the Mississippi,
Department #2 (August-November 1862)
Gardner's-Deas' Brigade, Withers'-Hindman's Division, 1st Corps, Army of
Tennessee (November 1862-November 1863)
Deas' Brigade, Hindman's-Anderson's-Johnson's-D. H. Hill's Division, 2nd
Corps, Army of Tennessee (November 1863-April 1865)

Battles: Murfreesboro (December 31, 1862-January 3, 1863)
Tullahoma Campaign (June 1863)
Chickamauga (September 19-20, 1863)
Chattanooga Siege (September-November 1863)
Chattanooga (November 23-25, 1863)
Atlanta Campaign (May-September 1864)
New Hope Church (May 25-June 4, 1864)
Peach Tree Creek (July 20, 1864)
Atlanta (July 22, 1864)
Ezra Church (July 28, 1864)
Jonesboro (August 31-September 1, 1864)
Atlanta Siege (July-September 1864)
Franklin (November 30, 1864)
Nashville (December 15-16, 1864)
Carolinas Campaign (February-April 1865)
Kinston (March 7-10, 1865)
Bentonville (March 19-21, 1865)

172. ALABAMA 40TH INFANTRY REGIMENT

Organization: Organized at Mobile on May 16, 1862. Regiment surrendered
at Vicksburg, Mississippi, on July 4, 1863. Paroled there later in month. Those
not captured apparently served in a temporary organization called Stone's
Sharpshooters Battalion. Declared exchanged in November 1863. Field consolidation with the 37th and 42nd Infantry Regiments in early 1865. Surren-

dered by General Joseph E. Johnston at Durham Station, Orange County, North Carolina, on April 26, 1865.

First Commander: Augustus A. Coleman (Colonel)

Field Officers: Ezekiel S. Gulley (Major, Lieutenant Colonel)
John H. Higley (Lieutenant Colonel, Colonel)
Thomas O. Stone (Major, Lieutenant Colonel)

Assignments: Army of Mobile, Department of Alabama and West Florida (October-November 1862)
Provisional Division, 2nd Military District, Department of Mississippi and East Louisiana (December 1862-January 1863)
Unattached, 2nd Military District, Department of Mississippi and East Louisiana (January 1863)
Moore's Brigade, Maury's Division, 2nd Military District, Department of Mississippi and East Louisiana (January-April 1863)
Moore's Brigade, Maury's-Forney's Division, Department of Mississippi and East Louisiana (April-July 1863)
Moore's Brigade, Cheatham's Division, 1st Corps, Army of Tennessee (November 1863-February 1864)
Moore's-Baker's Brigade, Stewart's-Clayton's Division, 2nd Corps, Army of Tennessee (February-September 1864)
Baker's Brigade, District of the Gulf, Department of Alabama, Mississippi and East Louisiana (September-October 1864)
Baker's Brigade, Liddell's Division, District of the Gulf, Department of Alabama, Mississippi and East Louisiana (October 1864-January 1865)
Baker's Brigade, Clayton's Division, 2nd Corps, Army of Tennessee (January-April 1865)

Battles: Chickasaw Bayou (December 27-29, 1862)
vs. Steele's Bayou Expedition (March 14-27, 1863)
Fore's Plantation (March 25, 1863)
Greenville Expedition (April 2-25, 1863)
Vicksburg Campaign (May-July 1863)
Vicksburg Siege (May-July 1863)
Chattanooga Siege (September-November 1863)
Chattanooga (November 23-25, 1863)
Atlanta Campaign (May-September 1864)
Rocky Face Ridge (May 5-11, 1864)
Resaca (May 14-15, 1864)
New Hope Church (May 25-June 4, 1864)
Atlanta (July 22, 1864)
Ezra Church (July 28, 1864)
Atlanta Siege (July-September 1864)

Carolinas Campaign (February-April 1865)
Bentonville (March 19-21, 1865)
Further Reading: Willett, Elbert Decatur. *History of C. B. (Originally Pickens Planters) 40th Alabama Regiment Confederate States Army.*

173. ALABAMA 41ST INFANTRY REGIMENT

Organization: Organized and mustered into Confederate service for three years or the war at Tuscaloosa on May 16, 1862. Surrendered at Appomattox Court House, Virginia, on April 9, 1865.

First Commander: Henry Talbird (Colonel)

Field Officers: Lemuel T. Hudgings (Major)
John M. Jeffries (Major)
Porter King (Lieutenant Colonel)
James T. Murfee (Lieutenant Colonel)
Jesse G. Nash (Major)
Martin L. Stanel (Major, Lieutenant Colonel, Colonel)
Theodore G. Trimmier (Major, Lieutenant Colonel)
Henry A. Whiting (Lieutenant Colonel)

Assignments: Department of East Tennessee (July-October 1862)
1st Brigade, Breckinridge's Division, 1st Corps, Army of Tennessee (November-December 1862)
Hanson's-Wright's Brigade, Breckinridge's Division, 2nd Corps, Army of Tennessee (December 1862-May 1863)
Kentucky Brigade, Breckinridge's Division, Department of the West (May-July 1863)
Kentucky Brigade, Breckinridge's Division, Department of Mississippi and East Louisiana (July-August 1863)
Kentucky Brigade, Breckinridge's Division, 2nd Corps, Army of Tennessee (September-November 1863)
Gracie's Brigade, Buckner's Division, 1st Corps, Army of Tennessee (November 1863)
Gracie's Brigade, Buckner's Division, Department of East Tennessee (November 1863-May 1864)
Gracie's Brigade, Department of Richmond (May-June 1864)
Gracie's Brigade, Johnson's Division, Department of North Carolina and Southern Virginia (July-October 1864)
Gracie's-Moody's Brigade, Johnson's Division, 4th Corps, Army of Northern Virginia (October 1864-April 1865)

Battles: Murfreesboro (December 31, 1862-January 3, 1863)
Tullahoma Campaign (June 1863)
Jackson Siege (July 1863)

Chickamauga (September 19-20, 1863)
Chattanooga Siege (September-November 1863)
Knoxville Siege (November 1863)
Chester Station (May 10, 1864)
Petersburg Siege (June 1864-April 1865)
The Crater (July 30, 1864)
Appomattox Court House (April 9, 1865)

174. ALABAMA 42ND INFANTRY REGIMENT

Organization: Organized and mustered into Confederate service for three years or the war at Columbus, Mississippi, on May 16, 1862. Surrendered at Vicksburg, Mississippi, on July 4, 1863. Paroled there later in month. Declared exchanged in November 1863. Field consolidation with the 37th and 40th Infantry Regiments from November 1864 to early 1865. Consolidated with the 37th and 54th Infantry Regiments and designated as the 37th Infantry Regiment Consolidated at Smithfield, North Carolina, on April 9, 1865.

First Commander: John W. Portis (Colonel)
Field Officers: W. C. Fergus (Major)
Thomas C. Lanier (Lieutenant Colonel, Colonel)
Assignments: Moore's Brigade, Maury's Division, Army of West Tennessee, Department #2 (September-October 1862)
Moore's Brigade, Maury's Division, Price's Corps, Army of West Tennessee, Department of Mississippi and East Louisiana (October 1862-January 1863)
Moore's Brigade, Maury's-Forney's Division, 2nd Military District, Department of Mississippi and East Louisiana (January-April 1863)
Moore's Brigade, Forney's Division, Department of Mississippi and East Louisiana (April-July 1863)
Moore's Brigade, Cheatham's Division, 1st Corps, Army of Tennessee (November 1863-February 1864)
Moore's-Baker's Brigade, Stewart's-Clayton's Division, 2nd Corps, Army of Tennessee (February-September 1864)
Baker's Brigade, District of the Gulf, Department of Alabama, Mississippi and East Louisiana (September-October 1864)
Baker's Brigade, Liddell's Division, District of the Gulf, Department of Alabama, Mississippi and East Louisiana (October 1864-January 1865)
Baker's Brigade, Clayton's Division, 2nd Corps, Army of Tennessee (January-April 1865)
Battles: Corinth (October 3-4, 1862)
vs. Yazoo Pass Expedition (February 3-April 10, 1863)
Vicksburg Campaign (May-July 1863)
Port Gibson (May 1, 1863)

Champion Hill (May 16, 1863)
Vicksburg Siege (May-July 1863)
Chattanooga Siege (September-November 1863)
Chattanooga (November 23-25, 1863)
Atlanta Campaign (May-September 1864)
Rocky Face Ridge (May 5-11, 1864)
Resaca (May 14-15, 1864)
New Hope Church (May 25-June 4, 1864)
Atlanta (July 22, 1864)
Ezra Church (July 28, 1864)
Atlanta Siege (July-September 1864)
Carolinas Campaign (February-April 1865)

175. ALABAMA 43RD INFANTRY REGIMENT

Organization: Organized and mustered into Confederate service for three years or the war at Mobile on May 15, 1862. Surrendered at Appomattox Court House, Virginia, on April 9, 1865.

First Commander: Archibald Gracie, Jr. (Colonel)

Field Officers: Thomas M. Barbour (Major)
Robert D. Hart (Major)
John J. Jolly (Lieutenant Colonel)
William J. Mims (Major)
Young M. Moody (Lieutenant Colonel, Colonel)

Assignments: Leadbetter's Brigade, Heth's Division, Department of East Tennessee (July-October 1862)
Gracie's Brigade, Heth's Division, Department of East Tennessee (October-November 1862)
Gracie's Brigade, Department of East Tennessee (December 1862-September 1863)
Gracie's Brigade, Preston's Division, Buckner's Corps, Army of Tennessee (September-October 1863)
Gracie's Brigade, Buckner's Division, 1st Corps, Army of Tennessee (October-November 1863)
Gracie's Brigade, Buckner's Division, Department of East Tennessee (November 1863-May 1864)
Gracie's Brigade, Department of Richmond (May-June 1864)
Gracie's Brigade, Johnson's Division, Department of North Carolina and Southern Virginia (July-October 1864)
Gracie's-Moody's Brigade, Johnson's Division, 4th Corps, Army of Northern Virginia (October 1864-April 1865)

Battles: Chickamauga (September 19-20, 1863)

Chattanooga Siege (September-November 1863)
Knoxville Siege (November 1863)
Bean's Station (December 14, 1863)
Chester Station (May 10, 1864)
Petersburg Siege (June 1864-April 1865)
The Crater (July 30, 1864)
Appomattox Court House (April 9, 1865)

176. ALABAMA 44TH INFANTRY REGIMENT

Organization: Organized at Selma on May 16, 1862. Surrendered at Appomattox Court House, Virginia, on April 9, 1865.

First Commander: James Kent (Colonel)

Field Officers: George W. Cary (Major)

Charles A. Derby (Lieutenant Colonel, Colonel)

John A. Jones (Major, Lieutenant Colonel)

William F. Perry (Major, Lieutenant Colonel, Colonel)

Assignments: Wright's Brigade, Huger's Division, Army of Northern Virginia (June-July 1862)

Wright's Brigade, Anderson's Division, 1st Corps, Army of Northern Virginia (July-November 1862)

Law's Brigade, Hood's Division, 1st Corps, Army of Northern Virginia (November 1862-February 1863)

Law's Brigade, Hood's Division, Department of North Carolina and Southern Virginia (February-April 1863)

Law's Brigade, Hood's Division, Department of Southern Virginia (April-May 1863)

Law's Brigade, Hood's Division, 1st Corps, Army of Northern Virginia (May-September 1863)

Law's Brigade, Hood's Division, Longstreet's Corps, Army of Northern Virginia (September-November 1863)

Law's Brigade, Hood's-Field's Division, Department of East Tennessee (November 1863-April 1864)

Law's-Perry's Brigade, Field's Division, 1st Corps, Army of Northern Virginia (April 1864-April 1865)

Battles: Seven Days Battles (June 25-July 1, 1862)

2nd Bull Run (August 28-30, 1862)

Malvern Hill (July 1, 1862)

Antietam (September 17, 1862)

Fredericksburg (December 13, 1862)

Washington, North Carolina (March 30-April 14, 1863)

Suffolk Campaign (April-May 1863)

Battery Huger (Companies A and B) (April 19, 1863)
Gettysburg (July 1-3, 1863)
Chickamauga (September 19-20, 1863)
Chattanooga Siege (September-November 1863)
Wauhatchie (October 28-29, 1863)
Knoxville Siege (November 1863)
The Wilderness (May 5-6, 1864)
Spotsylvania Court House (May 8-21, 1864)
North Anna (May 23-26, 1864)
Cold Harbor (June 1-3, 1864)
Petersburg Siege (June 1864-April 1865)
Fort Harrison (September 29-30, 1864)
Fort Gilmer (September 29-30, 1864)
Appomattox Court House (April 9, 1865)

177. ALABAMA 45TH INFANTRY REGIMENT

Organization: Organized at Auburn on May 19, 1862. Companies D and H had been part of the 34th Infantry Regiment. Field consolidation with the 16th and 33rd Infantry Regiments from the fall of 1864 to April 8, 1865. Consolidated with the 1st (apparently), 16th and 33rd Infantry Regiments at Smithfield, North Carolina, on April 8, 1865.

First Commander: William S. Goodwyn (Colonel)

Field Officers: Robert H. Abercrombie (Major, Lieutenant Colonel)
Ephraim B. Breedlove (Major, Lieutenant Colonel, Colonel)
George C. Freeman (Major)
James C. Gilchrist (Lieutenant Colonel, Colonel)
Harris D. Lampley (Major, Lieutenant Colonel, Colonel)

Assignments: 2nd Brigade, 2nd Corps, Army of the Mississippi, Department #2 (June-July 1862)
2nd Brigade, 2nd Division, Army of the Mississippi, Department #2 (July 1862)
3rd Brigade, 2nd Division, Army of the Mississippi, Department #2 (August 1862)
3rd Brigade, 2nd Division, Left Wing, Army of the Mississippi, Department #2 (August-November 1862)
Walthall's Brigade, Anderson's Division, 2nd Corps, Army of Tennessee (November-December 1862)
Anderson's Brigade, Withers' Division, 1st Corps, Army of Tennessee (December 1862-January 1863)
Wood's-Lowrey's Brigade, Cleburne's Division, 2nd Corps, Army of Tennessee (April-November 1863)

Lowrey's Brigade, Cleburne's Division, 1st Corps, Army of Tennessee (November 1863-April 1865)

Battles: Perryville (October 8, 1862)
Murfreesboro (December 31, 1862-January 3, 1863)
Tullahoma Campaign (June 1863)
Chickamauga (September 19-20, 1863)
Chattanooga Siege (September-November 1863)
Chattanooga (November 23-25, 1863)
Atlanta Campaign (May-September 1864)
Resaca (May 14-15, 1864)
New Hope Church (May 25-June 4, 1864)
Kennesaw Mountain (June 27, 1864)
Peach Tree Creek (July 20, 1864)
Atlanta (July 22, 1864)
Atlanta Siege (July-September 1864)
Jonesboro (August 31-September 1, 1864)
Spring Hill (November 29, 1864)
Franklin (November 30, 1864)
Nashville (December 15-16, 1864)
Carolinas Campaign (February-April 1865)

178. ALABAMA 46TH INFANTRY REGIMENT

Organization: Organized at Loachapoka on May 20, 1862. Surrendered at Vicksburg, Mississippi, on July 4, 1863. Paroled there later in month. Declared exchanged in November 1863. Consolidated with the 23rd and 31st Infantry Regiments and designated as the 23rd Infantry Regiment Consolidated at Smithfield, North Carolina, on April 9, 1865.

First Commander: Michael L. Woods (Colonel)

Field Officers: George E. Brewer (Major)
James M. Handley (Major)
Osceola Kyle (Lieutenant Colonel)

Assignments: Taylor's Brigade, Stevenson's Division, Department of East Tennessee (June 1862)
Post of Chattanooga, Department of East Tennessee (June-July 1862)
Taylor's Brigade, Stevenson's Division, Department of East Tennessee (July-October 1862)
Tracy's Brigade, McCown's Division, Department of East Tennessee (October-December 1862)
Tracy's Brigade, 2nd Military District, Department of Mississippi and East Louisiana (December 1862-January 1863)

Tracy's Brigade, Stevenson's Division, 2nd Military District, Department of Mississippi and East Louisiana (January-April 1863)
Tracy's-Garrott's-Lee's Brigade, Stevenson's Division, Department of Mississippi and East Louisiana (April-July 1863)
Pettus' Brigade, Stevenson's Division, 1st Corps, Army of Tennessee (November 1863-February 1864)
Pettus' Brigade, Stevenson's Division, 2nd Corps, Army of Tennessee (February 1864-April 1865)

Battles: Cumberland Gap (June 18, 1863)
Vicksburg Campaign (May-July 1863)
Port Gibson (May 1, 1863)
Champion Hill (May 16, 1863)
Vicksburg Siege (May-July 1863)
Chattanooga Siege (September-November 1863)
Chattanooga (November 23-25, 1863)
Atlanta Campaign (May-September 1864)
New Hope Church (May 25-June 4, 1864)
Atlanta (July 22, 1864)
Atlanta Siege (July-September 1864)
Jonesboro (August 31-September 1, 1864)
Franklin (not engaged) (November 30, 1864)
Nashville (December 15-16, 1864)
Carolinas Campaign (February-April 1865)
Bentonville (March 19-21, 1865)

179. ALABAMA 47TH INFANTRY REGIMENT

Organization: Organized and mustered into Confederate service for three years at Loachapoka, on May 20, 1862. Surrendered at Appomattox Court House, Virginia, on April 9, 1865.
First Commander: James M. Oliver (Colonel)
Field Officers: Michael J. Bugler (Major, Lieutenant Colonel, Colonel)
James M. Campbell (Major)
James W. Jackson (Lieutenant Colonel, Colonel)
John Y. Johnston (Major)
Leigh R. Terrell (Lieutenant Colonel)
Assignments: Taliaferro's Brigade, Jackson's Division, 2nd Corps, Army of Northern Virginia (July 1862-January 1863)
Law's Brigade, Hood's Division, 1st Corps, Army of Northern Virginia (January-February 1863)
Law's Brigade, Hood's Division, Department of North Carolina and Southern Virginia (February-April 1863)

Law's Brigade, Hood's Division, Department of Southern Virginia (April-May 1863)

Law's Brigade, Hood's Division, 1st Corps, Army of Northern Virginia (May-September 1863)

Law's Brigade, Hood's Division, Longstreet's Corps, Army of Northern Virginia (September-November 1863)

Law's Brigade, Hood's-Field's Division, Department of East Tennessee (November 1863-April 1864)

Law's-Perry's Brigade, Field's Division, 1st Corps, Army of Northern Virginia (April 1864-April 1865)

Battles: 2nd Bull Run (August 28-30, 1862)
Antietam (September 17, 1862)
Fredericksburg (December 13, 1862)
Washington, North Carolina (March 30-April 14, 1863)
Suffolk Campaign (April-May 1863)
Gettysburg (July 1-3, 1863)
Chickamauga (September 19-20, 1863)
Chattanooga Siege (September-November 1863)
Wauhatchie (October 28-29, 1863)
Knoxville Siege (November 1863)
The Wilderness (May 5-6, 1864)
Spotsylvania Court House (May 8-21, 1864)
North Anna (May 23-26, 1864)
Cold Harbor (June 1-3, 1864)
Petersburg Siege (June 1864-April 1865)
Fort Harrison (September 29-30, 1864)
Fort Gilmer (September 29-30, 1864)
Appomattox Court House (April 9, 1865)

Further Reading: Botsford, T. F. *Memories of the War of Secession.* Botsford, T. F. *A Sketch of the Forty-seventh Alabama Regiment Volunteers,* C.S.A. Burton, Joseph Q. *Historical Sketches of the Forty-Seventh Alabama Infantry Regiment,* C.S.A.

180. ALABAMA 48TH INFANTRY REGIMENT

Organization: Organized at Auburn on May 22, 1862. Surrendered at Appomattox Court House, Virginia, on April 9, 1865.

First Commander: James L. Sheffield (Colonel)

Field Officers: Enoch Alldredge (Major)
Jessee J. Alldredge (Lieutenant Colonel)
William M. Hardwick (Major, Lieutenant Colonel)
Abner A. Hughes (Lieutenant Colonel)

Columbus B. St. John (Major)
John W. Wigginton (Major)

Assignments: Taliaferro's Brigade, Jackson's Division, 2nd Corps, Army of Northern Virginia (July 1862-January 1863)
Law's Brigade, Hood's Division, 1st Corps, Army of Northern Virginia (January-February 1863)
Law's Brigade, Hood's Division, Department of North Carolina and Southern Virginia (February-April 1863)
Law's Brigade, Hood's Division, Department of Southern Virginia (April-May 1863)
Law's Brigade, Hood's Division, 1st Corps, Army of Northern Virginia (May-September 1863)
Law's Brigade, Hood's Division, Longstreet's Corps, Army of Northern Virginia (September-November 1863)
Law's Brigade, Hood's-Field's Division, Department of East Tennessee (November 1863-April 1864)
Law's-Perry's Brigade, Field's Division, 1st Corps, Army of Northern Virginia (April 1864-April 1865)

Battles: 2nd Bull Run (August 28-30, 1862)
Harpers Ferry (September 12-15, 1862)
Antietam (September 17, 1862)
Fredericksburg (December 13, 1862)
Washington, North Carolina (March 30-April 14, 1863)
Suffolk Campaign (April-May 1863)
Gettysburg (July 1-3, 1863)
Chickamauga (September 19-20, 1863)
Chattanooga Siege (September-November 1863)
Wauhatchie (October 28-29, 1863)
Knoxville Siege (November 1863)
The Wilderness (May 5-6, 1864)
Spotsylvania Court House (May 8-21, 1864)
North Anna (May 23-26, 1864)
Cold Harbor (June 1-3, 1864)
Petersburg Siege (June-April 1865)
Fort Harrison (September 29-30, 1864)
Fort Gilmer (September 29-30, 1864)
Appomattox Court House (April 9, 1865)

181. ALABAMA 49TH INFANTRY REGIMENT

Also Known As: Alabama 31st (Hale's) Infantry Regiment (in the field)

Organization: Organized as the 52nd Infantry Regiment at Nashville, Tennessee, on January 30, 1862. Reorganized as the 49th Infantry Regiment on May 8, 1862. Field consolidation with the 27th Infantry Regiment and 6th (Norwood's) Infantry Battalion from October 1862 to January 1863. Surrendered at Port Hudson, Louisiana, on July 8, 1863. Paroled in April 1864. Field consolidation with the 27th and 35th Infantry Regiments from July 1864 to April 9, 1865. Consolidated with the 27th, 35th, 55th and 57th Infantry Regiments at Smithfield, North Carolina, on April 9, 1865.

First Commander: Smith D. Hale (Colonel)

Field Officers: William N. Crump (Lieutenant Colonel)
Jeptha Edwards (Colonel)
Montgomery Gilbreath (Lieutenant Colonel)
B. C. Johnson (Major)
Thomas A. Street (Major)
John D. Weeden (Major, Lieutenant Colonel)

Assignments: Breckinridge's Brigade, Reserve, Central Army of Kentucky, Department #2 (February-March 1862)
Trabue's-Hawes' Brigade, Reserve Corps, Army of the Mississippi, Department #2 (March-June 1862)
Hawes' Brigade, Breckinridge's Command, District of the Mississippi, Department #2 (June-July 1862)
Helm's Brigade, Clark's Division, Breckinridge's Command, District of the Mississippi, Department #2 (July-August 1862)
Rust's Brigade, Lovell's Division, District of the Mississippi, Department #2 (October 1862)
(——— Brigade), Maury's Division, Army of West Tennessee, Department of Mississippi and East Louisiana (October-December 1862)
(——— Brigade), Rust's Division, 1st Corps, Army of North Mississippi, Department of Mississippi and East Louisiana (December 1862-January 1863)
Beall's Brigade, 3rd Military District, Department of Mississippi and East Louisiana (January 1863)
Buford's Brigade, 3rd Military District, Department of Mississippi and East Louisiana (March-April 1863)
Beall's Brigade, 3rd Military District, Department of Mississippi and East Louisiana (April-July 1863)
Post of Cahaba, Department of Mississippi and East Louisiana (January 1864)
Post of Cahaba, Department of Alabama, Mississippi and East Louisiana (January-May 1864)
Scott's Brigade, Loring's Division, Army of Mississippi (May-July 1864)

Scott's Brigade, Loring's Division, 3rd Corps, Army of Tennessee (July 1864-
April 1865)
Battles: Shiloh (April 6-7, 1862)
Corinth Campaign (April-June 1862)
Vicksburg Bombardments (May 18-27, 1862)
Baton Rouge (August 5, 1862)
Corinth (October 3-4, 1862)
Port Hudson Bombardment (March 14, 1863)
Port Hudson Siege (May-July 1863)
Atlanta Campaign (May-September 1864)
New Hope Church (May 25-June 4, 1864)
Peach Tree Creek (July 20, 1864)
Ezra Church (July 28, 1864)
Atlanta Siege (July-September 1864)
Jonesboro (August 31-September 1, 1864)
Franklin (November 30, 1864)
Nashville (December 15-16, 1864)
Carolinas Campaign (February-April 1865)

182. ALABAMA 50TH INFANTRY REGIMENT

Organization: Organized as the 26th (Coltart's) Infantry Regiment by the
consolidation of the 2nd (Davis'-Chadwick's) and 5th (Golladay's) Infantry
Battalions at Corinth, Mississippi, on April 3, 1862, per S.O. #27, 2nd Corps,
Army of the Mississippi, Department #2. Field consolidation with the 39th
Infantry Regiment from early 1863 to the summer of 1863. Designation
changed to the 50th Infantry Regiment on June 6, 1863, per S.O. #135,
Adjutant and Inspector General's Office. Consolidated with the 22nd, 25th
and 39th Infantry Regiments and designated as the 22nd Infantry Regiment
Consolidated at Smithfield, North Carolina, on April 9, 1865.

First Commander: John G. Coltart (Colonel)

Field Officers: George W. Arnold (Lieutenant Colonel)
William D. Chadwick (Lieutenant Colonel)
Newton N. Clements (Lieutenant Colonel)
Thomas H. Gilbert (Major)
Andrew D. Gwynne (Major)
John C. Hutto (Major)

Assignments: Gladden's-Gardner's Brigade, Withers' Division, 2nd Corps,
Army of the Mississippi, Department #2 (April-June 1862)
Gardner's Brigade, Reserve Corps, Army of the Mississippi, Department #2
(June-July 1862)

Gardner's Brigade, Reserve Division, Army of the Mississippi, Department #2 (July-August 1862)
Gardner's Brigade, Withers' Division, Right Wing, Army of the Mississippi, Department #2 (August-November 1862)
Gardner's-Deas' Brigade, Withers'-Hindman's Division, 1st Corps, Army of Tennessee (November 1862-November 1863)
Deas' Brigade, Hindman's-Anderson's-Johnson's-D. H. Hill's Division, 2nd Corps, Army of Tennessee (November 1863-April 1865)

Battles: Shiloh (April 6-7, 1862)
Corinth Campaign (April-June 1862)
Murfreesboro (December 31, 1862-January 3, 1863)
Tullahoma Campaign (June 1863)
Chickamauga (September 19-20, 1863)
Chattanooga Siege (September-November 1863)
Chattanooga (November 23-25, 1863)
Atlanta Campaign (May-September 1864)
New Hope Church (May 25-June 4, 1864)
Peach Tree Creek (July 20, 1864)
Atlanta (July 22, 1864)
Ezra Church (July 28, 1864)
Atlanta Siege (July-September 1864)
Franklin (November 30, 1864)
Nashville (December 15-16, 1864)
Carolinas Campaign (February-April 1865)
Kinston (March 7-10, 1865)
Bentonville (March 19-21, 1865)

183.   ALABAMA 52ND INFANTRY REGIMENT
See: ALABAMA 49TH INFANTRY REGIMENT

184.   ALABAMA 54TH INFANTRY REGIMENT
Organization: Organized by the assignment of Alabama companies (B, C, D, E, F and I) of the 4th Confederate Infantry Regiment and Companies A, E, H and K, 40th Tennessee Infantry Regiment, at Jackson, Mississippi, on October 9, 1862. Consolidated with the 37th and 42nd Infantry Regiments and designated as the 37th Infantry Regiment Consolidated at Smithfield, North Carolina, on April 9, 1865.
First Commander: Alpheus Baker (Colonel)
Field Officers: John A. Minter (Lieutenant Colonel, Colonel)
Thaddeus H. Shackelford (Major, Lieutenant Colonel)

Assignments: Baldwin's-Tilghman's Brigade, 1st Corps, Army of Mississippi, Department of Mississippi and East Louisiana (October 1862-January 1863)

Tilghman's Brigade, Loring's Division, Army of the Department of Mississippi and East Louisiana (January 1863)

Tilghman's Brigade, Loring's Division, Department of Mississippi and East Louisiana (January-April 1863)

Buford's Brigade, Loring's Division, Department of Mississippi and East Louisiana (April-May 1863)

Buford's Brigade, Department of the West (May-July 1863)

Buford's Brigade, Loring's Division, Department of Mississippi and East Louisiana (July 1863-January 1864)

Buford's Brigade, Loring's Division, Department of Alabama, Mississippi and East Louisiana (January-March 1864)

Provost guard duty at Montgomery (March-April 1864)

Baker's Brigade, Stewart's-Clayton's Division, 2nd Corps, Army of Tennessee (May-September 1864)

Baker's Brigade, District of the Gulf, Department of Alabama, Mississippi and East Louisiana (September-October 1864)

Baker's Brigade, Liddell's Division, District of the Gulf, Department of Alabama, Mississippi and East Louisiana (October 1864-January 1865)

Baker's Brigade, Clayton's Division, 2nd Corps, Army of Tennessee (January-April 1865)

Battles: vs. Yazoo Pass Expedition (February 3-April 10, 1863)

Vicksburg Campaign (May-July 1863)

Champion Hill (May 16, 1863)

Jackson Siege (July 1863)

Meridian Campaign (February-March 1864)

Atlanta Campaign (May-September 1864)

Rocky Face Ridge (May 5-11, 1864)

Resaca (May 14-15, 1864)

New Hope Church (May 25-June 4, 1864)

Atlanta (July 22, 1864)

Ezra Church (July 28, 1864)

Atlanta Siege (July-September 1864)

Carolinas Campaign (February-April 1865)

185. ALABAMA 55TH INFANTRY REGIMENT

Organization: Organized by the consolidation of the 6th (Norwood's) and 16th (Snodgrass') Infantry Battalions at Port Hudson, Louisiana, on February 23, 1863. Consolidated with the 27th, 35th, 49th and 57th Infantry Regiments at Smithfield, North Carolina, on April 9, 1865.

First Commander: John Snodgrass (Colonel)
Field Officers: James B. Dickey (Major)
Neill S. Graham (Lieutenant Colonel)
Joseph H. Jones (Major)
Jonathan H. Norwood (Lieutenant Colonel)
Assignments: Buford's Brigade, 3rd Military District, Department of Mississippi and East Louisiana (March-April 1863)
Buford's Brigade, Loring's Division, Department of Mississippi and East Louisiana (April-May 1863)
Buford's Brigade, Loring's Division, Department of the West (May-July 1863)
Buford's Brigade, Loring's Division, Department of Mississippi and East Louisiana (July 1863-January 1864)
Buford's-Scott's Brigade, Loring's Division, Department of Alabama, Mississippi and East Louisiana (January-May 1864)
Scott's Brigade, Loring's Division, Army of Mississippi (May-July 1864)
Scott's Brigade, Loring's Division, 3rd Corps, Army of Tennessee (July 1864-April 1865)
Battles: Vicksburg Campaign (May-July 1863)
Champion Hill (May 16, 1863)
Jackson Siege (July 1863)
Meridian Campaign (February-March 1864)
Atlanta Campaign (May-September 1864)
New Hope Church (May 25-June 4, 1864)
Peach Tree Creek (July 20, 1864)
Ezra Church (July 28, 1864)
Atlanta Siege (July-September 1864)
Jonesboro (August 31-September 1, 1864)
Franklin (November 30, 1864)
Nashville (December 15-16, 1864)
Carolinas Campaign (February-April 1865)

186. ALABAMA 57TH INFANTRY REGIMENT

Also Known As: Alabama 54th Infantry Regiment
Organization: Organized at Troy on April 13, 1863. Consolidated with the 27th, 35th, 49th and 55th Infantry Regiments at Smithfield, North Carolina, on April 9, 1865.
First Commander: John P. W. Amerine (Colonel)
Field Officers: William C. Bethune (Lieutenant Colonel)
Charles J. L. Cunningham (Major, Lieutenant Colonel)
James W. Mabrey (Lieutenant Colonel)
James H. Wiley (Major)

Assignments: Slaughter's Brigade, Department of the Gulf (June 1863)
Eastern Division, District of the Gulf, Department of Alabama, Mississippi and
   East Louisiana (July-September 1863)
Clanton's Brigade, Department of the Gulf (September 1863-February 1864)
Scott's Brigade, Loring's Division, Department of Alabama, Mississippi and
   East Louisiana (March-May 1864)
Scott's Brigade, Loring's Division, Army of Mississippi (May-July 1864)
Scott's Brigade, Loring's Division, 3rd Corps, Army of Tennessee (July 1864-
   April 1865)
Battles: Atlanta Campaign (May-September 1864)
New Hope Church (May 25-June 4, 1864)
Peach Tree Creek (July 20, 1864)
Ezra Church (July 28, 1864)
Atlanta Siege (July-September 1864)
Jonesboro (August 31-September 1, 1864)
Franklin (November 30, 1864)
Nashville (December 15-16, 1864)
Carolinas Campaign (February-April 1865)
Bentonville (March 19-21, 1865)

187. ALABAMA 58TH INFANTRY REGIMENT

Organization: Organized by the addition of Company E, 2nd (Cox's) Georgia
Sharpshooters Battalion, to the 9th Infantry Battalion (2nd Organization) on
June 28, 1863. Officially designated as the 58th Infantry Regiment on August
13, 1863. Field consolidation with the 32nd Infantry Regiment from November
24, 1863, to May 4, 1865. Surrendered by Lieutenant General Richard Taylor,
commanding the Department of Alabama, Mississippi and East Louisiana, at
Meridian, Mississippi, on May 4, 1865.
First Commander: Bushrod Jones (Colonel)
Field Officers: John W. Inzer (Lieutenant Colonel)
Harry I. Thornton (Major)
Assignments: Bate's Brigade, Stewart's Division, 2nd Corps, Army of Ten-
   nessee (June-September 1863)
Bate's Brigade, Stewart's Division, Buckner's Corps, Army of Tennessee (Sep-
   tember-October 1863)
Bate's Brigade, Stewart's Division, 2nd Corps, Army of Tennessee (October-
   November 1863)
Clayton's-Holtzclaw's Brigade, Stewart's-Clayton's Division, 2nd Corps, Army
   of Tennessee (November 1863-January 1865)
Holtzclaw's Brigade, District of the Gulf, Department of Alabama, Mississippi
   and East Louisiana (January-April 1865)

Holtzclaw's Brigade, Department of Alabama, Mississippi and East Louisiana
(April-May 1865)
Battles: Chickamauga (September 19-20, 1863)
Chattanooga Siege (September-November 1863)
Chattanooga (November 23-25, 1863)
Atlanta Campaign (May-September 1864)
Rocky Face Ridge (May 5-11, 1864)
Resaca (May 14-15, 1864)
New Hope Church (May 25-June 4, 1864)
Kennesaw Mountain (June 27, 1864)
Atlanta (July 22, 1864)
Ezra Church (July 28, 1864)
Atlanta Siege (July-September 1864)
Columbia (November 29, 1864)
Franklin (November 30, 1864)
Nashville (December 15-16, 1864)
Mobile (March 17-April 12, 1865)
Spanish Fort (April 2-8, 1865)

188. ALABAMA 59TH INFANTRY REGIMENT

Organization: Organized by the consolidation of the 2nd Infantry Battalion,
Hilliard's Legion, and the 4th Artillery Battalion, Hilliard's Legion, at Charleston on November 25, 1863. Surrendered at Appomattox Court House, Virginia, on April 9, 1865.
First Commander: Bolling Hall, Jr. (Colonel)
Field Officers: Lewis H. Crumpler (Major)
George W. Huguley (Major, Lieutenant Colonel)
John D. McLennan (Lieutenant Colonel)
Assignments: Gracie's Brigade, Buckner's Division, Department of East Tennessee (November 1863-May 1864)
Gracie's Brigade, Department of Richmond (May-June 1864)
Gracie's Brigade, Johnson's Division, Department of North Carolina and
Southern Virginia (July-October 1864)
Gracie's Brigade, Johnson's Division, 4th Corps, Army of Northern Virginia
(October 1864-April 1865)
Battles: Knoxville Siege (November 1863)
Bean's Station (December 15, 1863)
Dandridge (December 24, 1863)
Chester Station (May 10, 1864)
Drewry's Bluff (May 16, 1864)
Petersburg Siege (June 1864-April 1865)

The Crater (July 30, 1864)
Hatcher's Run (February 5-7, 1865)
White Oak Road (March 31, 1865)
Appomattox Court House (April 9, 1865)
Further Reading: Davidson, William H. *Word From Camp Pollard.*

189. ALABAMA 60TH INFANTRY REGIMENT
Organization: Organized by the consolidation of the 3rd and four companies of the 1st Infantry Battalions, Hilliard's Legion, at Charleston on November 25, 1863. Surrendered at Appomattox Court House, Virginia, on April 9, 1865.
First Commander: John W. A. Sanford (Colonel)
Field Officers: Hatch Cook (Major)
Daniel S. Troy (Lieutenant Colonel)
Assignments: Gracie's Brigade, Buckner's Division, Department of East Tennessee (November 1863-May 1864)
Gracie's Brigade, Department of Richmond (May-June 1864)
Gracie's Brigade, Johnson's Division, Department of North Carolina and Southern Virginia (July-October 1864)
Gracie's Brigade, Johnson's Division, 4th Corps, Army of Northern Virginia (October 1864-April 1865)
Battles: Knoxville Siege (November 1863)
Bean's Station (December 15, 1863)
Dandridge (December 24, 1863)
Chester Station (May 10, 1864)
Drewry's Bluff (May 16, 1864)
Petersburg Siege (June 1864-April 1865)
The Crater (July 30, 1864)
Hatcher's Run (February 5-7, 1865)
White Oak Road (March 31, 1865)
Appomattox Court House (April 9, 1865)
Further Reading: Shaver, Lewellyn A. *A History of the Sixtieth Alabama Regiment, Gracie's Alabama Brigade.*

190. ALABAMA 61ST INFANTRY REGIMENT
Also Known As: Alabama 59th Infantry Regiment
Organization: Organized as a battalion of nine companies at Pollard on May 2, 1863. Increased to a regiment on April 11, 1864. Surrendered at Appomattox Court House, Virginia, on April 9, 1865.
First Commander: William G. Swanson (Colonel)
Field Officers: Neill S. Graham (Lieutenant Colonel)
Lewis H. Hill (Major, Lieutenant Colonel)

William E. Pinckard (Major)

Assignments: Eastern Division, Department of the Gulf (September 1863)
Clanton's Brigade, Department of the Gulf (September 1863-January 1864)
Battle's Brigade, Rodes' Division, 2nd Corps, Army of Northern Virginia
  (February-June 1864)
Battle's Brigade, Rodes'-Grimes' Division, Valley District, Department of
  Northern Virginia (June-December 1864)
Battle's Brigade, Grimes' Division, 2nd Corps, Army of Northern Virginia
  (December 1864-April 1865)

Battles: The Wilderness (May 5-6, 1864)
Spotsylvania Court House (May 8-21, 1864)
North Anna (May 23-26, 1864)
Cold Harbor (June 1-3, 1864)
Lynchburg Campaign (June 1864)
Monocacy (July 9, 1864)
3rd Winchester (September 19, 1864)
Fisher's Hill (September 22, 1864)
Cedar Creek (October 19, 1864)
Petersburg Siege (from December 1864) (June 1864-April 1865)
Fort Stedman (March 25, 1865)
Appomattox Court House (April 9, 1865)

Further Reading: Davidson, William H. *Word From Camp Pollard.*

191. ALABAMA 62ND INFANTRY REGIMENT

Organization: Organized by the change of designation of the 1st Infantry
  Regiment Reserves in March 1865. Captured at Fort Blakely on April 9,
  1865. Exchanged later in month. Surrendered by Lieutenant Richard Taylor,
  commanding the Department of Alabama, Mississippi and East Louisiana, at
  Citronelle, Alabama, on May 4, 1865.

First Commander: Daniel E. Huger (Colonel)

Field Officers: James L. Davidson (Lieutenant Colonel)
Bruno F. Yniestra (Major)

Assignments: Thomas' Brigade, District of the Gulf, Department of Alabama,
  Mississippi and East Louisiana (March-April 1865)
Department of Alabama, Mississippi and East Louisiana (April-May 1865)

Battles: Mobile (March 17-April 12, 1865)
Spanish Fort (April 2-8, 1865)
Fort Blakely (April 1-9, 1865)

192.   ALABAMA 63RD INFANTRY REGIMENT

Organization: Organized by the change of designation of the 2nd Infantry Regiment Reserves in March 1865. Surrendered at Fort Blakely on April 9, 1865. Exchanged later in month. Surrendered by Lieutenant Richard Taylor, commanding the Department of Alabama, Mississippi and East Louisiana, at Citronelle, Alabama on May 4, 1865.
First Commander: Olin F. Rice (Colonel)
Field Officers: John H. Echols (Major)
Junius A. Law (Lieutenant Colonel)
Assignments: Thomas' Brigade, District of the Gulf, Department of Alabama, Mississippi and East Louisiana (March-April 1865)
Department of Alabama, Mississippi and East Louisiana (April-May 1865)
Battles: Mobile (March 17-April 12, 1865)
Spanish Fort (April 2-8, 1865)
Fort Blakely (April 1-9, 1865)

193.   ALABAMA 65TH INFANTRY REGIMENT

Organization: Organized by the consolidation of the 3rd and 4th Infantry Battalions Reserves in March 1865. Captured at Girard on April 16, 1865.
Assignments: Clanton's Brigade, District of the Gulf, Department of Alabama, Mississippi and East Louisiana (March-April 1865)
Department of Alabama, Mississippi and East Louisiana (April 1865)
Battles: Mobile (March 17-April 12, 1865)
Wilson's Raid (March 22-April 24, 1865)

194.   ALABAMA HILLIARD'S LEGION

Organization: Organized with three infantry, one artillery and one cavalry battalion at Montgomery on June 25, 1862. 5th Cavalry Battalion transferred to the 10th Confederate Cavalry Regiment on December 30, 1862. Broken up and divided as the 59th and 60th Infantry Regiments and the 23rd Sharpshooters Battalion on November 25, 1863.
First Commander: Henry W. Hilliard (Colonel)
Field Officers: A. H. Bradford (Colonel)
Jack Thorington (Colonel)
Further Reading: Shaver, Lewellyn A. *A History of the Sixtieth Alabama Regiment, Gracie's Alabama Brigade.*

195.   ALABAMA HILLIARD'S LEGION, 1ST INFANTRY BATTALION

Organization: Organized with seven companies at Montgomery on June 25, 1862. Four companies consolidated with the 3rd Infantry Battalion, Hilliard's

Legion, and designated as the 60th Infantry Regiment at Charleston on November 25, 1863. Remaining three companies became the 23rd Sharp-shooters Battalion.

First Commander: Jack Thorington (Lieutenant Colonel)

Field Officer: John H. Hot (Major, Lieutenant Colonel)

Assignments: 4th Brigade, McCown's Division, Department of East Tennessee (October-November 1862)

5th Brigade, Heth's Division, Department of East Tennessee (November 1862)

Palmer's Brigade, Department of East Tennessee (December 1862-March 1863)

Gracie's Brigade, Department of East Tennessee (April-September 1863)

Gracie's Brigade, Preston's Division, Buckner's Corps, Army of Tennessee (September-October 1863)

Gracie's Brigade, Buckner's Division, 1st Corps, Army of Tennessee (October-November 1863)

Battles: Chickamauga (September 19-20, 1863)

Chattanooga Siege (September-November 1863)

Further Reading: Shaver, Lewellyn A. *A History of the Sixtieth Alabama Regiment, Gracie's Alabama Brigade.*

196. ALABAMA HILLIARD'S LEGION, 2ND INFANTRY BATTALION

Organization: Organized with six companies at Montgomery on June 25, 1862. Consolidated with the 4th Artillery Battalion and designated as the 59th Infantry Regiment at Charleston, Tennessee on November 25, 1863.

First Commander: Bolling Hall, Jr. (Colonel)

Field Officer: William T. Stubblefield (Major)

Assignments: 4th Brigade, McCown's Division, Department of East Tennessee (October-November 1862)

5th Brigade, Heth's Division, Department of East Tennessee (November 1862)

Gracie's Brigade, Department of East Tennessee (December 1862-March 1863)

Gracie's Brigade, Department of East Tennessee (April-September 1863)

Gracie's Brigade, Preston's Division, Buckner's Corps, Army of Tennessee (September-October 1863)

Gracie's Brigade, Buckner's Division, 1st Corps, Army of Tennessee (October-November 1863)

Battles: Chickamauga (September 19-20, 1863)

Chattanooga Siege (September-November 1863)

Further Reading: Shaver, Lewellyn A. *A History of the Sixtieth Alabama Regiment, Gracie's Alabama Brigade.*

197. ALABAMA HILLIARD'S LEGION, 3RD INFANTRY BATTALION

Organization: Organized with six companies at Montgomery on June 25, 1862. Consolidated with four companies of the 1st Infantry Battalion, Hilliard's Legion, and designated as the 60th Infantry Regiment at Charleston on November 25, 1863.

First Commander: John W. A. Sanford (Colonel)

Field Officers: Hatch Cook (Major)

Daniel S. Troy (Major)

Assignments: 4th Brigade, McCown's Division, Department of East Tennessee (October-November 1862)

5th Brigade, Heth's Division, Department of East Tennessee (November 1862)

Knoxville, Department of East Tennessee (December 1862-March 1863)

Gracie's Brigade, Department of East Tennessee (April-September 1863)

Gracie's Brigade, Preston's Division, Buckner's Corps, Army of Tennessee (September-October 1863)

Gracie's Brigade, Buckner's Division, 1st Corps, Army of Tennessee (October-November 1863)

Battles: Chickamauga (September 19-20, 1863)

Chattanooga Siege (September-November 1863)

Further Reading: Shaver, Lewellyn A. *A History of the Sixtieth Alabama Regiment, Gracie's Alabama Brigade.*

198. ALABAMA HILLIARD'S LEGION, 4TH ARTILLERY BATTALION

Organization: Organized with five companies at Montgomery on June 25, 1862. Consolidated with the 5th Infantry Battalion, Hilliard's Legion, and designated as the 59th Infantry Regiment at Charleston on November 25, 1863.

First Commander: William N. Reeves (Major, Lieutenant Colonel)

Field Officer: John D. McLennan (Major)

Assignments: 4th Brigade, McCown's Division, Department of East Tennessee (October-November 1862)

5th Brigade, Heth's Division, Department of East Tennessee (November 1862)

Palmer's Brigade, Department of East Tennessee (December 1862-March 1863)

Gracie's Brigade, Department of East Tennessee (April-September 1863)

Gracie's Brigade, Preston's Division, Buckner's Corps, Army of Tennessee (September-October 1863)

Gracie's Brigade, Buckner's Division, 1st Corps, Army of Tennessee (October-November 1863)

Battles: Chickamauga (September 19-20, 1863)

Chattanooga Siege (September-November 1863)
Further Reading: Shaver, Lewellyn A. *A History of the Sixtieth Alabama Regiment, Gracie's Alabama Brigade.*

199. ALABAMA HILLIARD'S LEGION, 5TH CAVALRY BATTALION

Organization: Organized with five companies at Montgomery on June 25, 1862. Merged into the 10th Confederate Cavalry Regiment on December 30, 1862.
First Commander: Miles M. Slaughter (Major)
Assignments: 4th Brigade, McCown's Division, Department of East Tennessee (October-November 1862)
5th Brigade, Heth's Division, Department of East Tennessee (November 1862)

200. ALABAMA LOCKHART'S INFANTRY BATTALION

Organization: Organized with nine companies in 1864. Company F became Company K, 8th (Ball's-Hatch's) Cavalry Regiment. Increased to a regiment and designated as the 1st Infantry Regiment Reserves in August 1864.
First Commander: Harrison C. Lockhart (Lieutenant Colonel)
Field Officer: James L. Davidson (Major)

201. ALABAMA STONE'S INFANTRY BATTALION SHARPSHOOTERS

Organization: Organized in the summer of 1863 from those members of the 40th Infantry Regiment not captured at Vicksburg, Mississippi. Rejoined their proper commands upon the exchange of the balance of the regiment in November 1863.
First Commander: Thomas O. Stone (Lieutenant Colonel)
Assignment: Ector's Brigade, Walker's, Reserve Corps, Army of Tennessee (September-November 1863)
Battles: Chickamauga (September 19-20, 1863)
Chattanooga Siege (September-November 1863)

BIBLIOGRAPHY

Amman, William. *Personnel of the Civil War.* 2 volumes. New York: Thomas Yoseloff, 1961. Provides valuable information on local unit designations, general officers' assignments and organizational data on geographical commands.

Boatner, Mark Mayo III. *The Civil War Dictionary.* New York: David McKay Company, 1959. Provides thumbnail sketches of leaders, battles, campaigns, events and units.

Bowman, John S. *The Civil War Almanac.* New York: Facts On File, 1982. Basically a chronology; it is valuable for its 130 biographical sketches, many of them military personalities.

Daniel, Larry J. *Cannoneers in Gray: The Field Artillery of the Army of Tennessee, 1861-1865.* University, Ala.: University of Alabama Press, 1984. An excellent study of the artillery in the western theater.

Evans, Clement A., ed. *Confederate Military History.* 13 volumes. Atlanta: Confederate Publishing Company, 1899. Each volume of this series primarily provides the histories of one or two states. Each state military account was written by a different participant in the war, and they vary greatly in quality. All accounts, however, include biographies of the generals from their state. The lack of a comprehensive index is the major drawback of this work. Volume XII includes an Alabama chapter by Lieutenant General Joseph Wheeler that contains comprehensive unit histories.

Freeman, Douglas Southall. *Lee's Lieutenants: A Study in Command.* 3 volumes. New York: Charles Scribner's Sons, 1941-1946. The premier narrative study of the organizational and command structure of the Army of Northern Virginia.

————. *R. E. Lee: A Biography.* 4 volumes. New York: Charles Scribner's Sons, 1934-1935. Also provides organizational information on the Army of Northern Virginia.

Johnson, Robert Underwood, and Buel, Clarence Clough, eds. *Battle and Leaders of the Civil War.* 4 volumes. New York: The Century Company, 1887.

Reprinted 1956. Exceptionally valuable for its tables of organization for major engagements.

Krick, Robert K. *Lee's Colonels: A Biographical Register of the Field Officers of the Army of Northern Virginia*, 2nd edition. Dayton, Ohio: Press of Morningside Bookstore, 1984. Brief but very informative sketches of the 1,965 field-grade officers who at one time or another served with the Army of Northern Virginia but never achieved the rank of brigadier general. The second edition also includes a listing by name and unit of those field-grade officers who never served with Lee.

Long, E. B., and Barbara. *The Civil War Day by Day: An Almanac 1861-1865*. Garden City, N.Y.: Doubleday, 1971. An excellent chronology of the conflict, with much information on the organizational changes command assignments.

Lonn, Ella. *Foreigners in the Confederacy*. Chapel Hill: University of North Carolina, 1940. Accounts of the foreign-born contribution to the Confederacy.

National Archives, Record Group 109. Microfilm compilation of the service records of every known Confederate soldier, organized by unit. The caption cards and record-of-events cards at the beginning of each unit provide much valuable information on the units' organizational history.

Scharf, J. Thomas. *History of the Confederate States Navy: From Its Organization to the Surrender of Its Last Vessels*. Albany: Joseph McDonough, 1887. A rather disjointed narrative that provides some insight into operations along the southern coast and on the inland waterways. Unfortunately, it lacks an adequate index.

Sifakis, Stewart. *Who Was Who in the Civil War*. New York: Facts On File, 1988.

———. *Who Was Who in the Confederacy*. New York: Facts On File, 1989. Together, both works include biographies of over 1,000 participants who served the South during the Civil War. The military entries include much information on regiments and higher commands.

U.S. Navy Department. *Official Records of the Union and Confederate Navies in the War of the Rebellion*. 31 volumes. Washington: Government Printing Office, 1894-1927. Provides much valuable information on the coastal and riverine operations of the Civil War.

U.S. War Department. *The War of the Rebellion: A Compilation of the Official Records of the Union and Confederate Armies*. 70 volumes in 128 books divided into four series, plus Atlas. Washington: Government Printing Office, 1881-1901. While difficult to use, this set provides a gold mine of information. Organized by campaigns in specified geographic regions, the volumes are divided into postaction reports and correspondence. The information contained in the hundreds of organizational tables proved invaluable for my purposes.

Wakelyn, Jon L. *Biographical Dictionary of the Confederacy.* Westport, Conn.: Greenwood Press, 1977. Short biographies of 651 leaders of the Confederacy. However, the selection criteria among the military leaders are somewhat haphazard.

Warner, Ezra J. *Generals in Gray: Lives of the Confederate Commanders.* Baton Rouge: Louisiana State University Press, 1959. Sketches of the 425 Southern generals. Good coverage of pre- and postwar careers. The wartime portion of the entries leaves something to be desired.

Wise, Jennings Cropper. *The Long Arm of Lee: The History of the Artillery of the Army of Northern Virginia.* Lynchburg, Va.: J. P. Bell Co., 1915. Reprinted 1959. An excellent study of Lee's artillery, providing valuable information on batteries and their commanders and organizational assignments.

Wright, Marcus J. *General Officers of the Confederate Army.* New York: Neale Publishing Co., 1911. Long the definitive work on the Confederate command structure, it was superseded by Ezra J. Warner's work.

PERIODICALS

Civil War Times Illustrated, its predecessor *Civil War Times, American History Illustrated* and *Civil War History.* In addition, the *Southern Historical Society Papers* (47 vols., 1876-1930) are a gold mine of information on Confederate units and leaders.

BATTLE INDEX

References are to record numbers, not page numbers.

1st Bull Run, Virginia 112, 118, 121
1st Winchester, Virginia 134
2nd Bull Run, Virginia 112, 115, 124, 127, 129, 130, 133, 134, 176, 179, 180
3rd Winchester, Virginia 106, 118, 121, 131, 190

Ackworth, Georgia 156
Adairsville, Georgia 136
Aiken 45
Antietam, Maryland 24, 25, 106, 112, 115, 118, 121, 124, 127, 129, 130, 131, 132, 133, 134, 154, 176, 179, 180
Appomattox Court House, Virginia 24, 25, 106, 112, 115, 118, 121, 124, 127, 129, 130, 131, 132, 133, 134, 148, 173, 175, 176, 179, 180, 188, 189, 190
Atlanta, Georgia 29, 35, 44, 45, 62, 71, 73, 95, 136, 138, 141, 143, 146, 149, 153, 160, 161, 163, 164, 167, 168, 170, 171, 172, 174, 177, 178, 182, 184, 187
Atlanta Campaign 9, 14, 16, 17, 19, 20, 21, 23, 29, 32, 34, 35, 37, 41, 44, 45, 48, 49, 50, 51, 56, 62, 69, 71, 72, 73, 95, 136, 137, 138, 141, 142, 143, 146, 149, 151, 153, 154, 156, 158, 159, 160, 161, 163, 164, 165, 166, 167, 168, 170, 171, 172, 174, 177, 178, 181, 182, 184, 185, 186, 187
Atlanta Siege 14, 16, 17, 19, 20, 21, 23, 29, 32, 34, 37, 41, 44, 45, 48, 49, 50, 51, 56, 62, 69, 71, 72, 73, 95, 136, 137, 138, 141, 142, 143, 146, 149, 151, 153, 154, 156, 158, 159, 160, 161, 163, 164, 165, 166, 167, 168, 170, 171, 172, 174, 177, 178, 181, 182, 184, 185, 186, 187
Averasboro, North Carolina 63, 95

Baton Rouge, Louisiana 135, 166, 181
Battery Huger 176 [Companies A and B]
Bay Minette Creek 145
Bean's Station, Virginia 134, 148, 175, 188, 189
Beaver Dam Creek, Virginia 115
Bentonville, North Carolina 41, 45, 56, 63, 71, 95, 142, 143, 146, 149, 153, 156, 159, 160, 161, 171, 172, 178, 182, 186
Big Shanty, Georgia 41, 161

Boteler's Ford, Virginia 134
Bradyville, Tennessee 65
Brentwood, Tennessee 72
Brice's Crossroads 76, 84
Bridge Creek, Mississippi 32
Bridgeport and Battle Creek 163
Bristoe Campaign, Virginia 25, 115, 118, 121, 124, 127, 129, 130, 132, 133, 154
Bristoe Station, Virginia 24
Buzzard Roost Gap, Georgia 136

Campbellton, Georgia 62
Carolinas Campaign 41, 44, 45, 56, 62, 63, 69, 71, 72, 73, 95, 96, 136, 138, 139, 142, 143, 144, 146, 149, 150, 151, 152, 153, 154, 156, 157, 158, 159, 160, 161, 164, 166, 168, 169, 171, 172, 174, 177, 178, 181, 182, 184, 185, 186
Cassville, Georgia 35, 136, 138, 141, 142
Cedar Creek, Virginia 106, 118, 121, 131, 190
Cedar Mountain, Virginia 115, 134
Champion Hill, Mississippi 12 [detachment], 36, 143, 149, 156, 160, 161, 166, 168, 174, 178, 184, 185

NAME INDEX

References are to record numbers, not page numbers.

Abercrombie, Robert H. 96, 177
Adams, Samuel 164
Aiken, James 132
Alexander, G. L. 135
Alldredge, Enoch 180
Alldredge, Jessee J. 180
Allen, William W. 41
Allston, Benjamin 112
Amerine, John P. W. 168, 186
Anderson, Charles D. 145
Andrews, William G. 31
Armistead, Edward H. 146
Armistead, Robert B. 146
Arnold, George W. 182
Arrington, Thomas M. 161
Ashe, Thomas P. 163
Ashford, Alva E. 166
Ashford, Frederic A. 136

Baine, David W. 133
Baker, Alpheus 184
Baker, Benjamin F. 121
Ball, Elias P. 54
Barbiere, Joseph 74
Barbour, Thomas M. 175
Battle, Cullen A. 106
Beall, Thaddeus S. 40
Beck, Franklin K. 149
Beckham, Robert F. 25
Bellamy, Richard H. 17
Bennett, Albert G. 62
Bethune, William C. 186
Betts, William H. 132
Bibb, Joseph B. 149, 150

Blackford, Eugene 118
Blakely, David T. 41
Blount, Robert P. 125
Bondurant, James W. 25
Bowles, Pickney D. 112
Boyles, William 66, 73
Bradford, A. H. 194
Bradford, Henry C. 100
Bradford, Taul 129, 160
Breedlove, Ephraim B. 177
Brewer, George E. 178
Brooks, William M. 108
Broome, James A. 133
Brown, John C. 131
Brown, Thomas B. 41
Bryan, David F. 154
Buck, William A. 151
Bugler, Michael J. 179
Bulger, William D. 108
Bullock, Edward C. 141
Burnett, Thomas J. 138
Burr, William H. 160
Burtwell, John R. B. 61
Butler, William L. 158
Byrd, William M. 113

Caldwell, John H. 129
Campbell, James M. 179
Campbell, Robert M. 6
Cantey, James 134
Carpenter, John N. 44
Carter, John C. 152, 165
Carter, Richard W. 44
Cary, George W. 176
Cary, Joseph M. 4
Cayce, Stewart W. 98, 145

Chadwick, William D. 99, 182
Chancellor, John L. 54
Charpentier, Stephen 9
Clanton, James H. 41
Clanton, Turner, Jr. 52
Clanton, N. H. 28
Clark, John W. 20
Clark, Whitfield 171
Clayton, Henry D. 95, 171
Clements, Newton N. 182
Clifton, James M. 109
Clifton, William C. 171
Coleman, Augustus A. 172
Coleman, Thomas K. 112
Coltart, John G. 103, 122, 182
Colvin, Charles H. 51
Conoley, John F. 159
Conoley, Jonathan F. 110
Cook, Hatch 189, 197
Crawford, James 145
Crittenden, Robert F. 164
Crow, James M. 127
Crump, William N. 181
Crumpler, Lewis H. 188
Cruse, Samuel R. 37
Culver, Isaac F. 121
Cunningham, Arthur S. 129
Cunningham, Charles J. L. 186
Cunningham, James 44

Daniel, John W. L. 134
Davidson, James L. 97, 191, 200

STEWART SIFAKIS, a free-lance writer on American historical topics, has been a Civil War enthusiast since childhood. He was a student of history and politics at George Washington University and the American College in Paris. Sifakis is the author of *Who Was Who in the Civil War* (Facts On File) and a longtime member of the Civil War Round Table of New York. Originally from Kew Gardens, New York, Sifakis currently resides in Zermatt, Switzerland.